WOODCARVING
A Complete Course

by Ron Butterfield

*GUILD OF MASTER CRAFTSMAN
PUBLICATIONS LTD*

DEDICATION
*To My Dear Wife Audrey, whose care and
understanding has been my unfailing support
over many years.*

ISBN 0 946819 04 1

Copyright © Guild of Master Craftsman Publications Ltd 1987.

*First published in 1987 by
Guild of Master Craftsman Publications Ltd
166 High Street, Lewes, Sussex BN7 1XU
England
Reprinted 1989.*

*Designed by
Madeline Serre.*

*Typeset by
CST Eastbourne, Sussex.*

*Printed by Richard Clay Ltd
Bungay, Suffolk.*

Contents

Introduction

Of recent years the increase in leisure time, earlier retirement and the trend towards a greater interest in, and the general appreciation of, traditional skills have all contributed to the rise of interest in woodcarving. As a part-time teacher of the subject for a great many years in Adult Further Education Centres until my retirement in 1985, this trend was very noticeable.

My students who came from all walks of life to attend these evening classes, objected strongly to them coming to an end. They found that it was possible to hire the classroom and continue as a carving 'club'. A club was formed and tuition continues.

To take a piece of wood and by using one's imagination and a few simple tools, give that material a special meaning and identity can be fascinating and rewarding.

Many people think the visual arts are the products of some kind of 'magic wand' granted to certain individuals and maybe to a degree they have a point. However, the old adage '10% inspiration, 90% perspiration' still applies and art or craft in any form requires instruction, study and the practical use of one's hands.

The range of carving in wood is immense, extending from the very simplest to the most advanced work, from decoration in the various historical styles to realistic or abstract sculpture.

The most important requirement when considering taking up the subject is the 'desire to do'. Provided that desire is present the actual techniques of carving, knowledge of timbers suitable for carving and design as applied to the subject of woodcarving can be imparted by this book.

The ability to produce work which is more correctly termed sculpture depends upon the individual. However, this can be acquired and happens more frequently than would be generally supposed. During my 37 or so years of teaching many students have become quite proficient at sculpture (woodcarving 'in the round').

What I can do here is attempt to open the door to the

Reproduced with kind permission of The Star, Sheffield.

Pages 4 & 5
The author at work carving the Eagle
Lectern for St Peter's Church, Ropsley,
Nr Grantham, Lincs.

world of 'form' and try to encourage readers to see the wonders of our natural world with the eye of a potential carver or sculptor. Be that as it may, woodcarving can also provide a very enjoyable and interesting pastime for young and old alike. Its requirements are such that anyone can have a try at the subject.

Acknowledgement

To J.W. Etchell, Jim to his staff. For many years Head of the Adult Education Centre, Rowlinson Campus, Sheffield.

He was the person who encouraged me to develop the subject of woodcarving and sculpture in the Adult Education Centre.

Bibliography

On the practical aspects of woodcarving:
One of the first books on woodcarving I ever read and one which I still consider to be very good indeed is *Woodcarving* by Alan Durst who taught woodcarving at the Royal College of Art for some time.

It was first published in 1938 by Studio Books of London and was a title in their 'How To Do It' series. It was re-printed in 1945 and a revised edition was pubished in 1959. According to my knowledge, it was last re-printed in 1961.

On Design, General and Applied Ornament
One of the best books is also one of the oldest. It is *Meyer's Handbook*, or to give it its full title: *A Handbook of Ornament* by Franz Sales Meyer.

First published in 1894 by B.T. Batsford, this book is a veritable treasure trove. My copy came to me years ago as a kind of heirloom.

To these can be added *Collins Guide to the Parish Churches of England and Wales* by John Betjeman. Collins. This is a fairly recent issue.

Also by John Betjeman along with Basil Clarke there is *English Churches* published in 1964 by Studio Vista. *Cathedrals of England* by Alec Clifton-Taylor, Book Club Associates 1972, from Thames & Hudson 1967 and others by the same author can also be recommended.

Among old publications, a treasure is *English Church Woodwork* by Howard E. Crossley. This again is a Batsford publication by subscribers dated 1917. This is still a gem. My own copy is another heirloom.

DRAWING AND DESIGN

Drawing is the basis of all art and in many crafts also, the ability to express one's ideas in the form of lines on paper is a great help. Drawing encourages one to really look at things with a seeing eye.

Years ago circa 1950, in the days of District Evening Schools, before the enormous and complex Adult Education Centres of today, I taught the general art subjects of drawing, painting and design for a few years.

Students in those classes commented then on the fact that they had never really looked at things until they started drawing them. Drawing also helps to stimulate the visual memory, helping it to retain shapes and images of things seen.

Even if you consider yourself unable to draw very well, try carrying a small pocket sketch book about with you. It need not be of extensive paper and failing a book a pad of paper such as used in photo-copiers takes pencil-line very well and can be used on a clip-board.

If you prefer a book, there are sketch-books available of Bond paper which is quite alright for either pen or pencil drawings. These come in a range of sizes, the A6 size 148 × 105mm 5.7/8 × 4.1/8 inches, fits easily into a pocket or handbag.

Use a soft rather than a hard-grade pencil; an HB or 1B or even a slightly softer lead will be easier to use than any of the 'H' grades for drawing and design. These latter pencils are best used when transferring the drawn design to the wood in use. They do tend to give a thinner line which is sharper and clear when used with carbon paper.

I personally find that to use a good quality pencil adds pleasure to the whole process. There are many excellent makes of pencil available now.

To begin, try sketches of leaves, Sycamore or Maple which are palmate in shape. There are leaves of all shapes to try.

Animals, birds, figures and faces can all provide ideas. When you draw such things try to keep them simple in shape, do not strive for excessive detail. If details interest you, draw

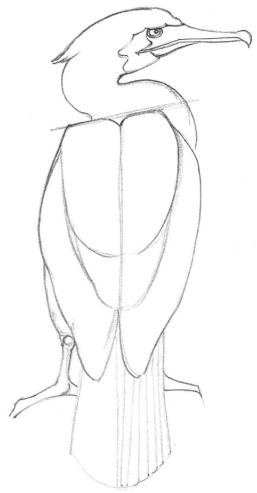

Fig. 1. Making sketches of subjects as ideas for carving projects helps stimulate the visual memory. This pencil study of a Cormorant concentrates on the bird's shape and proportions. Details can be added later or drawn separately.

Fig. 2. Many wild flowers and other plants can furnish ideas which would adapt to a carving design. The five petals of a cinque-foil offer scope in more rounded form.

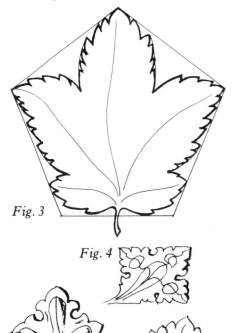

Fig. 3

Fig. 4

Fig. 5

Fig. 6

Fig. 3. A sycamore leaf fits into the geometric shape of a pentagon. Figs 4, 5 & 6 are variations on the shape of vine leaves found in many examples of medieval carving. Fig. 7 shows Bryony, the wild climbing plant, which would also adapt for a carving design.

studies of these on separate sheets or possibly at the side of your main drawings. Doing this will encourage you to observe your subject even closer.

Also, if for example a leaf has a geometrical basic shape, draw that in lightly first. Such a basis is found in a Sycamore leaf for example, the palmate shape of this fits into a pentagon, a five-sided figure. If you draw this geometric shape first the leaf is merely a development of this.

Other leaves having this pentagonal basis are the 'hop' and the humble 'vegetable marrow', indeed the latter makes an excellent subject for a decorative leaf.

Various leaves were used in medieval times, perhaps the most popular and certainly the most important one with this geometric basis was that of the vine.

The vine is of course a symbol of the Eucharist in the Christian church. A glance at the project on carving such a vine-leaf later on in this volume will show that the shape used is merely a variation on the theme.

The pentagon has been pulled out a little, giving extra length to the two edges which diverge from the line forming the base, this time having at its centre the stem of the leaf.

Other aspects of the subject of design will be dealt with as and when they occur relative to the various projects in the book.

This approach of basic shapes first will encourage the eye to view things as a design. Remember that whatever you draw, it is to provide information to use when preparing a design for carving.

Do not however, restrict your attempts at drawing to the above mentioned things only. Draw anything which you find of interest, the more you practise the better you will become at the subject.

It may help when drawing things for use as future carvings to try to analyse the shapes, possibly by suggesting the section-shape through the subject at various places. Do this in your studies or even in the main drawings. Explore the way a thing is made, think of its component parts. The more you understand such things, the more knowledge you will bring to your carvings.

Fig. 7

Fig. 8. The author seen working on the Crucified Christ. The Hanging Rood for the Parish Church of St. John Troedyrhiw.

Carvings are not solely essays in the use of certain tools, they would be sadly lacking in any creative content if they were.

Later on in the book when more advanced work is considered, the approach to three-dimensional form will be dealt with in more detail but the above ideas on drawing and design will help provide a basis for those later developments.

Fig. 3 shows the sycamore leaf developed from the suggested pentagonal base. Once you have made a start on the practical task of woodcarving these observations on drawing will become more relevant to you as a result of using the tools involved in carving.

Your designs will benefit from your experience in finding out just what the various chisels, gouges, etc., actually do and what effect is achieved by their usage.

Remember that practice, though it may not yet make quite perfect, will at least improve your abilities and skill.

SUITABLE TIMBERS

Wood has been used by man since the earliest times. It is a very versatile material and has been put to a great many uses in the course of the development of mankind.

A living material, it responds to a sympathetic treatment. It is not the carver's job to beat the wood into submission but to approach it with respect. Each species and type of timber has its own characteristics and these should be respected at all times. If this is done, the material will respond and give of its best. The carver or indeed any other craftsmen in wood should work with these characteristics, not against them.

Below are listed a few of the great many species of wood available to the artist-craftsman.

Hardwoods

Abura: Comes in the main from Nigeria and West Africa. It is a rather featureless wood, light in colour but with some variation. It has an even-texture, is straight grained and once seasoned is stable. It will carve but responds best to very sharp tools.

Afrormosia: From Ghana and the Ivory Coast of Africa. It is slow to season but is very stable once this state is achieved. A strong and durable timber, yellowish brown to a reddish brown in colour. In the paler forms it may have a greenish tinge, it looks a little like Teak and has a good figure. It did not come on to the market generally until after the 1939-45 war. It is fairly easy to carve but is not really suitable for work where a naturalistic style is to be attempted.

Agba: From West Africa where it grows to a great height. Pale in colour, varying from a straw colour to a pale-pinkish tint. Is stable once seasoned and is light in weight. Will carve but should not be used for anything which will come in contact with food.

Apple: Is generally available only in small diameters and sometimes the trunk of such trees may be misshapen. Hard and close-grained it carves well and will take small detail. An excellent timber for carving.

Ash: Can be carved but is more generally used where its great tensile strength is an asset.

Beech: Is excellent for carving and has a good colour. The grain has a fleck which adds interest.

Blackwood: From Africa and Australia. The latter is a member of the Acacia family and is an attractive timber of interesting colour. A golden to mid-brown with darker markings and has a reasonably straight grain. Sometimes this can be wavy giving an interesting colour and figure. It can be carved but the colour variations would have to be considered in relation to the subject being carved.

African Blackwood is not of the same family, being usually thought of as being among the rosewood group. This is probably because of its colour which is dark brown to almost black. Not really to be classed as a good carving material.

The name **Boxwood** is sometimes used for several fine grained timbers, but strictly speaking it should refer to the Buxus species. This is found in Britain, Southern Europe and through Turkey into Iran. Never a large tree the wood is available in small sizes only. Requires careful drying but once seasoned is excellent for carving. It is hard and takes detail very well. It was used by the great German master woodcarvers.

Cherry: Like most fruitwoods carves well but is available only in small sizes.

Chestnut (Sweet): A bit like oak to look at but is lighter and is easier to carve.

Cypress: Has been developed as a Plantation Tree in South Africa, New Zealand and Australia. It is a pale yellow brown in colour but can have an interesting grain which can, with care, be used to good effect. I remember a shoal of fish I saw carved in this timber which was excellent.

Elm: This is a 'woolly' wood having cross-fibres which tie the grain. It can be carved but should not be used for delicate work. It requires a robust subject and treatment and responds best to very sharp tools. Because of its characteristics is good for mallet heads.

Wych Elm: is heavier and possibly easier to manage.

Japanese Elm: is the easiest to carve.

Holly: is white or greyish-white, has a fine even texture. It is best cut to small sizes before drying, because larger sizes tend to distort during the process. Carves reasonably well.

Hornbeam: A bit like Beech in appearance but is heavier, can be carved but is really better for turning.

Idigbo: from West Africa, comes in large diameters. However, the medium sizes yield better timber. It looks a bit like through and through oak but has not the grain interest of oak even when it is quarter sawn. It can be carved but is not one of the best types for this.

Iroko: from Africa is a big tree giving large yields of good cylindrical logs. Colour yellow-brown to deep-brown with a lighter coloured stripe. The grain can be awkward but the wood will carve with care.

Jelutong: From S.E. Asia grows very tall, is generally straight-grained and fine textured, seasons quickly and is stable. It will carve. Incidentally it exudes a latex in growth and is tapped for this. The latex is used in the manufacture of chewing gum!

Laburnum: Bright yellow when cut it darkens later to dark brown, the heartwood is darkest. Available in small sizes, it carves well but can be woolly.

Lignum Vitae: is the hardest and heaviest of woods. Can vary in colour from dark green in commercial use, through brown to black. Carves well and takes a high polish.

Lime: Called **Basswood** in America. It is one of the most amenable of timbers for carving. European lime is stronger being a little more akin to Sycamore in this respect. It carves very well indeed and if obtainable is certainly a good timber for beginners in woodcarving. Sometimes referred to as a 'dead' looking wood, it is not if treated well. The grain can be brought to life with the appropriate polish, please refer to the finishes section later in the book. (Page 23.)

Mahogany: covers a large group of timbers including **African**, **Brazilian**, **Cuban** and **Honduras**.

African is a red-brown colour and is of medium texture. It will carve, but has some interlocking grain giving a stripe to the figure of the wood. It therefore requires care and sharp tools at these parts. Persuasion, not brute force, is best here.

Brazilian: Carves well and is of good colour. I have used it often.

Cuban: sometimes referred to as 'Spanish mahogany' is the hardest but also the most beautiful, being a deep, dark red. It is becoming a

11

rarity now and was the mahogany used by the master cabinet makers of the 18th century. An excellent timber, hard, but which works like a dream, each gouge cut gleams with a surface polished from the tool-action. So please show this timber the respect due and should you ever come by any, do not attempt to carve it until your skill is enough to do it justice.

Honduras: is the palest in colour and is softer than Cuban. It is also the easiest to carve, takes colour well and can be gilded.

Mansonia: from West Africa is medium to dark brown in colour but may become a lighter shade as it ages. It has a straight grain, not a heavy wood it is strong for its weight. Is a little akin to teak in that the dust is liable to irritate the skin, eyes and throat if used over long periods. Carves reasonably well.

Maple: carves well, see Sycamore to which it is related.

Meranti: There are a number of timbers in this group. However, I cannot really recommend any of them for carving.

Oak: is a large and important family, each member having its own characteristic.

English Oak: is the hardest and by far the most cussed to work. None-the-less it is interesting, has the most beautiful figure of all oak and gives a great sense of achievement. When a carving in this timber is completed it gives one great satisfaction. The treatment should be broad and robust, do not strive for small detail. Many excellent carvings in oak can be seen in Britain but more will be said of these later in the book.

Japanese Oak: is much more responsive to tools and is thus much easier to carve. It has an interesting colour and grain.

American Oak: sometimes referred to as Red Oak is not as satisfying to carve as the above mentioned members of the tribe.

Padauk: from West Africa and there used to be imports of this timber from Burma but this has fallen off of latter years. It is of a dark red colour with sometimes a purple-red form appearing. Very strong and carves well, but I've found it responds better to the use of simple forms which show the colour and good surface finish possible, than to naturalistic detail.

Pear: is excellent for carving but is generally only available in smaller sizes. Varies in colour from pale pink to light brown, has a fine-texture and is fairly hard. Requires care when seasoning.

Plane: is similar to Sycamore but has a more pronounced fleck-figure. It carves reasonably well but does need care when seasoning as it has some tendency to distort.

Poplar: A pale coloured, slightly woolly wood which carves quite well with sharp tools.

Purpleheart: from South America is brown when first felled, but deepens to purple on exposure. On prolonged exposure this becomes a rich-brown. Stable, once dry it can be carved but does have a tendency to take the edge off tools. Takes a high polish and would probably respond better to a formalized treatment of subject rather than a naturalistic approach.

Rosewood: Mainly from India and Brazil but some does come from the Central and South American countries. It is hard to come by nowadays, will carve but does need care and persuasion before it gives of its best.

Sycamore: is as stated before akin to Maple and is found in many parts of the globe. It is of high density and is close-grained, carves well and will take detail. It is also probably the best wood to use for items having any connection with food, i.e. butter moulds or bread boards.

Teak: Many timbers are referred to as 'teak' but only one true teak exists. This, to give the descriptive part of its botanical name is 'grandis', Teak grandis. Usually brown in colour but this varies from pale to dark in shade. It seasons slowly but is stable when dry and is very durable. It does have an abrasive texture and is notorious for taking the edge of tools, both hand-tools and such things as planing machines. In carving treat it broadly using simple shapes. Do not strive for too fine a detail in this timber.

Walnut: is a name applied to quite a number of timbers, mainly because of figure. However the true members of the species carry the name Juglans before their descriptive botanical names.

English Walnut: growns to large sizes and is a very fine timber. It came to the fore as a material in the furniture of Queen Anne's time. The grain is beautiful and it carves well with care.

French Walnut: is of straighter grain, is milder and more easily cut. Carves well and is very good carving material being a little easier to deal with than the English variety.

African Walnut: is so named because of its grain but is not a true walnut being of the Lovoa designation. It will carve but the interlock of the grain needs care and persuasion.

Willow: a pale coloured wood similar looking to Poplar. Does carve but not one of the better timbers for this.

Yew: Though a conifer and as such should perhaps be classified as Softwood, it is not soft. It is a very beautiful timber, changing colour from red when cut to brown after long exposure. Paler coloured markings are to be found in some boards. The grain is very decorative in effect possibly because it is a slow growing timber which may affect the growth rings. It carves well and can be brought to a high finish.

We end our alphabetical list with **Zebrano** or African Zebrawood. This is a very decorative wood having as its name would suggest a stripey effect to the grain. A strong wood it responds well to hand-tools but again subject matter carved should take advantage of the colour characteristics.

There are many more carvable timbers, should any come your way, try them. Only by doing so will experience be gained.

Softwoods

These are the narrow-leaved coniferous species as opposed to the broad-leaved deciduous trees which are designated Hardwoods.

Many softwoods can be carved and some will take colour where this is required, but generally speaking they respond better to a whittling technique using knives. Should you wish to try with wood-carving gouges etc., tools having a longer bevel than is usual will help, any such tools have to be kept extra sharp too. It may seem queer to say that softwoods require sharper carving tools than most hardwoods but such is the case.

Kauri: Pine from New Zealand varies in colour from pale yellowish-brown to brown with a pinkish shade. Of late this species has been recovering from over-cutting in its native land and so little has been exported.

Larch: does cast its leaves in winter, is resinous with a conspicuous grain. It also has dry knots so all told is not to be advised as a carving material.

Parana Pine: from Brazil is straw-coloured tending at times to a pale-brown with occasional red streaks. Difficult to season because of its tendency to distort.

Pitch Pine: is strong and was used a lot in the 19th century, but it is really not a timber I can recommend. The conspicuous grain could be interesting, if you wish to experiment with the effects to be found when carving in this material, you could at least have a try.

Yellow Pine: In its best quality grade carves well, but remember to use sharp tools.

This suggestion of trying out could well apply to the softwood family in general.

TOOLS AND EQUIPMENT

Fig. 1. 'Setting-in' shows hand position and incline of the tool away from the subject perimeter.

'Setting-In'

Throughout the book, the author will refer to 'setting-in'. This means the selection from your tools of the gouges to fit the curves of the perimeter of the design. Make sure your tools are sharp before you start. The gouges are then used to establish the lines of the carving.

The tools used cover a great diversity of size, shape and section. The so-called 'sets' on sale are of little use, containing as they do tools which are rarely required and failing to include gouges which are constantly needed.

Woodcarving tools generally have a number stamped on the tool blade at the top near the tang.

No. 1 is a flat chisel. These do not have shoulders to the blades as in Joiners' chisels which are generally heavy in section compared to carving tools.

Should you have Joiners' flat chisels which are not too heavy when handled you may be able to use these as substitutes for No. 1.

Various widths of this are required. ¼in (6mm), ⅜in (9mm) and ¾in (19mm) will do as a basis.

No. 2 is a skew-chisel ground off at an angle and having one bevel. See illustration.

These tools are not a vital necessity at first; my own is ¼in (6mm) wide and is used for trimming the margins of designs and photographs more than for carving.

No. 3 is the first gouge. It has a very shallow section and comes in many widths.

This is a very useful tool and two or three widths, ⅜in (9mm), ½in (12mm) and ⅝in (15mm) will be useful.

No. 4 is slightly deeper and a ⅜in (9mm) wide one is very useful.

From **No. 4** the gouges deepen in section until No. 7 which is approximately semi-circular. After this gouges become 'U' shaped in section and are called fluters, or if small, veiners.

Large sizes of these are useful for removing wood quickly when roughing out a large subject in the 'round', but are not required by beginners.

All tools are prefixed by other numbers in addition to that indicating the section. 3703 would be a straight gouge, No. 3 in section. Other prefixes indicate curved gouge, spoon-gouge, back-bent, vee tools etc. To begin with only straight tools are required.

A beginner's list could be chosen from the following.

No. 1 (3701) flat chisel, ¼in (6mm), ⅜in (9mm) and ¾in (19mm) wide.

No. 3 First gouge section ⅜in (9mm) and ⅝in (15mm) wide.

No. 4 Gouge section ⅜in (9mm) and ⅝in (15mm) wide.

No. 5 Gouge section ½in (12mm) and ⅝in (15mm) wide.

No. 6 Gouge section ⅜in (9mm) and ⅝in (15mm) wide.

No. 7 Gouge section ¾in (19mm) and ⅝in (15mm) wide.

No. 39 parting tool (vee section 60°) ¼in (6mm) wide = 3739.

In parting tools the numbers are 3739, 3741, 3745 etc. Indicating various angles. 60° vee is best for general use.

The inclusion of a parting tool in beginners' tools was questioned once by an adult student, so make it optional. In place have a grounding tool or tools for assistance when dealing with the background of reliefs.

These are cranked chisels, see *fig. 6*, which come in various widths. The prefix is 3721, or 4031 if not wider than ½in (12mm) is required. They are also made in left and right-hand skew shapes which are handy for dealing with corners, leaf serrations and many other problems in backgrounds.

If you have the finances, the above tools in various widths, say Nos. 3 and 4 up to ¾in (19mm) will increase your range.

These basics can be added to as you gain experience. The work in hand often suggests additions; one comes to the point where the thought 'Now if only I had such a width a little deeper' crops up.

If tools required can be bought at such times your kit will grow with the additions, each of which you know you need.

Fig. 2. The author's bench top with some gouges and chisels lying in the opened tool roll mentioned on page 18. The area reserved for sharpening can be seen bottom right.

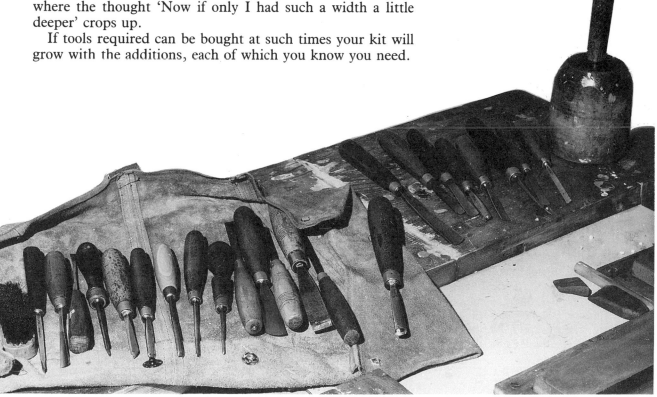

Fig. 4. Right: The full range of sweeps and sizes of London Pattern carving tools available from Ashley Iles Limited.

London Pattern Straight Gouges	London Pattern Curved Gouges	London Pattern Spoon Bit Gouges (Front Bent)	London Pattern Spoon Bit Gouges (Back Bent)	Fish Tail Pattern Straight Gouges	1/16" 1.5	3/32" 2.25	1/8" 3
3	12	24	33	54 x 3	—	—	⌣
4	13	25	34	54 x 4	—	—	⌣
5	14	26	35	54 x 5	—	—	⌣
6	15	27	36	54 x 6	—	—	⌣
7	16	28	37	54 x 7	—	⌣	⌣
8	17	29	38	54 x 8	⌣	⌣	⌣
9	18	30	–	54 x 9	∪	∪	∪
10	19	31	–	54 x 10	∪	∪	∪
11	20	32	–	54 x 11	∪	∪	∪

Fig. 3. Selection is made by reference to the tool Number above and opposite page and the chart of sizes and sweeps above right:
Reading from top to bottom:
No. 1 London Pattern straight chisel; No. 2 London Pattern straight corner chisel; Nos. 3 – 11 London Pattern straight gouge; Nos. 12 – 20 London Pattern curved gouge; No. 21 London Pattern spoon chisel; No. 22 London Pattern spoon chisel left-corner; No. 23 London Pattern spoon chisel right corner.

Fig. 5. (opposite page) Top to bottom: Nos. 24-32 London Pattern spoon gouge front bent; Nos. 39 – 46 London Pattern vee tool; Nos. 47 × 3 only, London Pattern grounding tool; No. 52 London Pattern dog leg chisel; Nos 33 – 38 London Pattern Spoon gouge back bent; No. 54 × 3 – 11 Fishtail Pattern gouge; No. 54 × 1 & 2 Fishtail Pattern chisel.

First attempts at animals or bird subjects bring the need for say, a smaller No. 5 or 6 perhaps ⅛in (3mm) or ³⁄₁₆in (4.5mm) wide. This would be used to carve the eyes. Only actual usage of tools imparts such needs.

I do find that some people approach the idea of buying tools with a 'one-upmanship' view. This attitude is often seen in the approach to other artistic hobbies and interests. The most expensive box of paints, either water colours or oils does not automatically produce the best pictures.

The Mallet, the one used by carvers, is very important and is *round* in section. There is a very practical reason for this. The mallet action becomes automatic, varying the strength of the blow according to the amount of wood to be removed at that instant.

Were a square section used the user would find his attention wandering to see if the square was slipping off the tool-handle and clouting his tool-hand.

This is obviated by the use of the round mallet and concentration can be kept where it should be, on the cutting edge of the tool and its action on the wood.

Timber for mallets, should you wish to make your own, are Beech or Elm, the former being the best in my opinion. Some talk is given to the use of Lignum Vitae, but I have one such

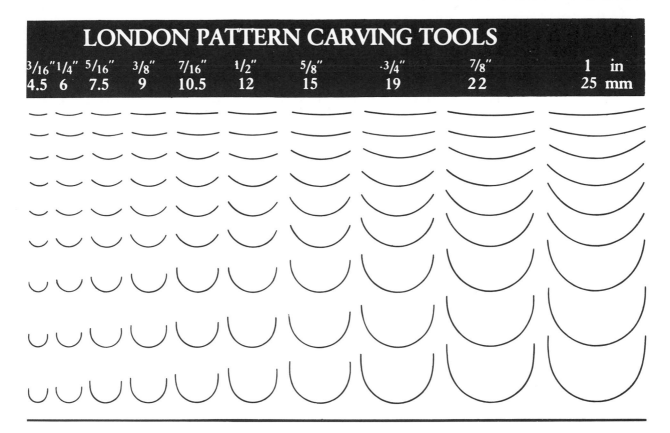

3/16"	1/4"	5/16"	3/8"	7/16"	1/2"	5/8"	-3/4"	7/8"	1	in
4.5	6	7.5	9	10.5	12	15	19	22	25	mm

LONDON PATTERN CARVING TOOLS

which is never used. Years ago I found a table leg, round in section and about 4in diameter at points along its length. Slices of this up to 4½in deep were cut and provided three good mallet-heads; the material Beech.

Handles – Ash is best for a mallet handle; for gouges etc., Ash or Beech. If you are very lucky you might find Boxwood handles.

My own range through many timbers – Ash to Rosewood. Many I have made myself, but the handles supplied by tool-makers are very good and are generally Beech or one of the Mahoganies.

One type I find odd are the plastic kind. Some sympathy or kinship can be generated by wooden handles; plastic for me is 'nil simpatico'.

Storage, care and carrying

Sharp tools present problems of storage. All hobbies lead to the accumulation of the things used therein and in woodcarving one tends to collect tools from many diverse sources. For myself many treasures have been found on the 'odds and ends' stalls found in country markets.

Woodwork tool-boxes of the usual kind are rather big and carving tools should not have to be delved-for in the dark

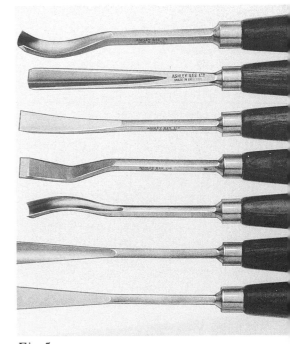

Fig. 5

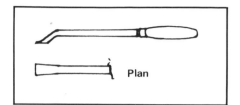

Fig. 6. A Grounding Tool is a type of cranked chisel most useful for dealing with backgrounds of relief work.

Fig. 7. Showing hand positions for maximum control over gouge when making fine cuts.

interiors of large boxes. Ideally they should be easily to hand at around table-top height or similar level and should not be jumbled up one upon another.

A cupboard with shelves of reasonable height from the ground upon which shallow boxes can be placed would be one possibility. The less bending necessary to find tools, the less wear and tear on one's back.

The bulk of my own tools are in a lidded box which can be locked and placed at a convenient height when opened for use.

It resembles a kind of suitcase made of wood with an interior of shallow trays of various sizes which can be lifted out. Under these, in the bottom of the case, are kept larger tools – gouges, fishtail chisels with wide cutting edges, large spoon-gouges and such. They tend to be the kind of tools used on comparatively rare occasions but which nevertheless have had to be available over the years in case they are needed.

The smaller of the trays are on slides so that each can be moved over to view the tools in the larger trays beneath.

I also have a very small chest with sliding trays in front of which a panelled front slots and locks. This is portable but is rarely so used. It contains especially precious, some indeed being almost miniature, tools. These could not be bought now, I doubt whether today's manufacturer's would have the swages required to make such tools.

Also keep in mind that tools should not be in collision, edges are soon damaged by tools being dropped one upon another in the box or case. Shallow wooden trays do enable the placing of tools in safe positions and also allow easier selection when the various ones are required. It is advisable if tools are to be left for any length of time without usage to lightly oil the blades. Handles will benefit from an occasional light waxing.

For carrying a selection of tools actually required for a specific carving, a toll rool is the best idea. They can be bought but over the years I have had to make a number for various purposes.

The tools are best arranged in a row in heads to tails positions. If the handles were all at one side the roll just would not roll – the bunch of handles becoming too bulky. Reversing the handles alternately lessens the effect. Rolls can be made from strong cloth or other materials, some of mine have been made from pieces of strong upholstery material acquired over the years.

The few tools I carried around in the army during the war were housed in a roll made from the strong canvas used by the coach trimmers for repairing the covers of 'soft-top' vehicles.

I made my present favourite from a discarded suede skirt passed on by one of my students. If you happen to have a robust piece of cloth rectangular in shape and you or your partner are handy with a needle and thread the job can be simplified.

18

Allow for flaps to fold over from top and bottom and have some arrangement for at least one end to also fold in. This will keep tools within the roll. Mine has a separate leather strap to fasten the roll when loaded with tools. But stitched ties of some strong material would serve just as well to encircle and fasten the roll in safety.

Sharpening equipment

This is a very important part of our subject; incorrect sharpening can ruin tools in no time.

There are many makes and grades of sharpening stones available. A rough or coarse grade may be required when dealing with new tools although nowadays some are sold in sharpened condition.

Generally speaking however, a combined stone having one side medium and the other fine grade will do quite well. I find it best to confine the sharpening process to one area of the bench top – see the notes on benches for more details.

Natural oilstones are expensive and hard to come by, the two main types are Washita and Arkansas. Both are from America. The best vein of White Washita, a very find grade stone is, I am told almost worked out. So if you should see such stones and have money to spare, get one.

Natural slipstones can be bought in various sizes and sections. They tend to be rather expensive, but if you can afford the money, treat yourself to two or three of different section shapes.

The object is to have slipstones with surfaces which will fit the inside curves of gouges, vee-tools etc. so that these can be used as described under 'Sharpening Methods'.

Should you be unable to purchase slipstones, but can lay your hands on a piece of slate say 9mm (⅜in) thick, the edges of this can be filed or ground to give curves to fit various gouges. Shape one edge to fit inside your parting tool with its v-section. By careful application, one section curve of a slipstone will do for tools of varying widths.

Some 'Sharpening Instructions' advocate an internal bevel to gouges. Different people have different ideas, but I do not encourage students to indulge in this rather inexplicable process.

Unsharpened new tools or those with broken or chipped cutting edges need a lot of attention. If you have a powered grindstone with medium or fine grade wheel, use this to reduce the cutting edge to a thickness you can deal with on your oilstone.

When using a powered grindstone, beware of 'blueing' the cutting edges of tools by too great or too prolonged pressure of the tool to the grindstone surface. Have a container of water nearby and constantly cool the tools' edges in this.

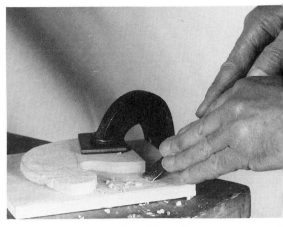

Fig. 8. Hand and tool position when finishing background surface, no mallet being used.

19

Fig. 9. Shows hand positions when dealing with a gouge of shallow section-curve, i.e. of section curvature less than No. 5 – 3705 straight gouge.

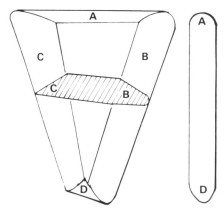

Fig 10. Slipstone with various edge-sections made by the author from a piece of dark grey slate. C – B shows section through at that point.

Sharpening methods

When sharpening tools, the outer bevel is placed on the surface of the stone and according to the depth of section, is passed 'to and fro' across the length of the stone, rolling the tool only sufficiently to bring all the width of the bevel into contact. Try to get a rythmic movement. Sections of No.'s 3 and 4 for example need less roll than No.'s 6 or 7 the section curves of which are much deeper.

Too much roll loses precious corners of the cutting edge. The object should be to have a slight curve to the cutting edge but keeping the outer corners square.

This process to the outer bevel produces a slight burr on the inner surface. This is called a 'wire-edge' by some. Find the slipstone with the curved surface appropriate to fit as near as possible the inside of the tool in question. Apply a small amount of oil to the slip surface and place this against the inner surface of gouge.

The oil used in sharpening is any good make of lubricating oil plus an amount of paraffin. There are proprietary brands available if you wish to purchase these.

Gently move the slipstone up and down against the inner surface. *Do not* tilt the stone. The object is merely to reduce the burr to a 'feather-edge', not to make any inside bevel.

The 'feather-edge' is then removed on a strop which is a small piece of leather used on the inside of the gouge. Eventually the 'feather' will come away leaving a very sharp tool, so watch your fingers.

Strops will become more effective if some dressing is applied to them. Not, I beseech you, with valve-grinding paste! No, a better idea is to give the strop a rub with tallow and then apply a light sprinkling of jeweller's rouge – 'crocus powder' as it is called in the silver trade.

The Bench

I have never had either the desire or the necessary finance to spare for the purchase of a work-bench. When asked to demonstrate at various venues 'Work-Mate' benches have sometimes been provided, but at the risk of upsetting the makers, I must say they do not greatly appeal.

The nucleus of my bench is a counter purchased from a small shop which was going out of business. The counter had originally been a knee-hole desk so you can see that it has had rather a chequered career.

The tier of drawers at the right-hand formed the basis from which the bench developed. The perspective impression gives some idea of the bench as it now stands.

Try to give proper consideration to working height; this is of prime importance.

My own bench is roughly 2ft 9in (84cm) high. When working full-time before retirement, the bench at the larger studio was higher than this but I now find the above height a reasonable one for comfort when working from a standing position.

Never having been really comfortable when standing for long periods at a stretch, when the work permits I sit. Here again the stool-height has developed over the years to that which is most comfortable.

The thing to remember is that the arrangement of bench size and lay-out is a matter of personal preference.

Should you be able to come by wood of a greater thickness for the top, use it. The legs also should be strong, those at the left-hand of the bench in the drawing are 105mm × 77mm (4in by 3in) approx.

The top and bottom rails are of this section and are halved in.

The two smaller drawers shown in the drawing can either be withdrawn or pushed in under the bench top. This allows the use of 'G' cramps when relief work or lettering is being cut. Also at this end, provision is made to receive the carver's 'chop' or vice.

The position of 'A' is covered by a piece of formica giving an easily cleaned surface on which sharpening equipment is arranged. Oil-stones of various grades are held in position by strips of wood screwed through the plastic and into the bench-top. Room is made for the oil-can, slipstones, strops, etc. and there is also the one water-stone I possess. This is of a very fine grade and is suitable for finishing prior to stropping.

Lighting

This is of prime importance. Natural light from a northern window is preferable wherever possible, however there are many occasions where natural light will have to be supplemented. Fluorescent lighting is not to be recommended, as a

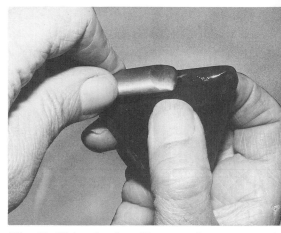

Fig. 11. Using the slate slipstone to hone the inside curve of a gouge.

Fig. 12. The author's bench. The two smaller drawers can either be withdrawn or pushed in under the top. This would allow the use of 'G' Cramps when relief work or lettering is being cut.

21

working light it does not reveal sufficiently the depth of cut being made.

The workroom will require a general light, but there are many adjustable task-lamps on the market which will give additional help.

Some task-lamps have screw-cramp fixings which can be positioned appropriately when bench-top thickness and over-hang will allow. Other lamps having a weighted base will stand either on the bench or adjacent to the working position.

Use a bulb of fairly high wattage, the actual power is best decided by individuals. Find the light and position of light which best suits you; experiment with types and positions.

Holding the work

This is important, never try to use sharp tools on an insecure piece of wood, to do so is to invite accidents.

'G' Cramps shaped as their name suggests are very good when used for holding work being carved in relief. These are available in a large range of sizes from 50mm (2in) to 300mm (12in) in capacity. They are strong and in the larger sizes can hold quite thick pieces of wood.

Bench holdfasts These hold work flat to the bench top and are available in adjustable and fixed versions. They consist of a stem with a cramping arm at an angle to this. The fixed types are made in one piece, but the adjustable versions are to be preferred. These also have a hinged shoe-piece allowing positioning on the wood surface to be more easily achieved.

The arm is hinged too and has a strong threaded adjustment to hold the shoe down firmly in position on the wood. This type is also supplied with a collar. Holes are requried to be made at intervals through the bench-top, into which the stem may be inserted. The collar is best let in at the top of the holes and to be flush with the bench surface. Failing this, it can be removed if a large piece of work requires this.

The carver's 'chop' or vice surmounts the bench-top and is made of wood with metal fittings. My own is quite old now, bought just after the last war.

The effective opening extends to 230mm (9in); has a depth to the thread of just over 105mm (4in) possibly the width of the gripping surfaces are also 4in.

The overall base length is 480mm (19in), by 100mm (4in) in width, with height to the top of the jaws of around 220mm (8½in). If this type is not available, a woodworker's vice, one of the various types available is quite suitable.

All vice-jaws will require some softening to be added to prevent any marking of the work in hand. My own has pieces of cork which are renewable when worn. Leather is sometimes used in 'chops' and softwood pieces are used generally with a woodworker's vice. A piece of softening must be used also under the holdfast-shoe or 'G' cramp grip.

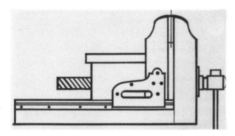

Fig. 13. A carver's 'Chop' or vice with quick-release is ideal for holding work being carved in the 'round'. Line the metal jaws with some timber suitable for softening.

Polishing and Finishing

There are various methods of polishing carvings when they are finished. One is with wax polish and plenty of elbow-grease.

White polish (shellac) used on all edges, ends, front and rear of a carving will seal the surface. When thoroughly dry, wax polish can be used and given a good rub with a duster. If dusted at intervals, the finish will improve with time.

French polish applied and then finished with a 'rubber' as in professional practice is not really suitable except when an abstract carving is produced. Abstract work often relies on a high surface finish for the best effect.

When carving wood for exhibition I sometimes use an oil polish. The recipe for this came to light in a very old book I came by in my early teens. It brings out the grain of the wood and enlivens the work.

The recipe is based on **boiled linseed oil** which is good for the wood to which it is applied. It feeds the material, brings out the colour and grain figuration and, if combined with other ingredients, makes an excellent polish.

Try mixing equal portions of boiled linseed oil, turpentine or white spirit and vinegar. Put these in a bottle or capped jar and give it a good shake.

The resulting emulsion should be applied to the completed carving with a clean brush, a new paint brush, for example.

Make sure that the liquid enters all crevices etc. of the carving. Leave until this has been absorbed and is dry, then apply a second coat. Leave this for around 12 hours and then give a third coat and after the same interval, wipe off any excess with a cotton rag.

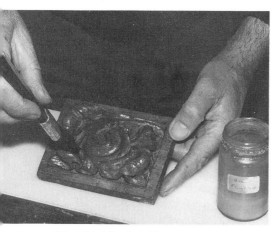

Fig. 14. The finishing treatment is an emulsion made up of Linseed Oil, Turpentine, and vinegar applied with clean brush.

Leave for a further drying period, looking at intervals to check the surface condition. Then give the whole of the surface a brisk rub with a clean, dry bristle-brush, a nail brush will do the job quite well. This helps to clear away any residue from the details of the carving.

After this, it is all a matter for dusters and elbow-grease. Make sure the dusters used are clean and give the carving a good rub. Continue this rubbing at intervals and the surface will begin to take on a pleasant finish. Wax polish can be applied later and rubbed well to complete the process.

With this polishing method it takes time to achieve results, but I find it worthwhile; the polish does improve with further waxing and rubbing. It also feeds and protects the wood.

Resin oil – from descriptions read, this should be a finishing material, but having never used it, I cannot speak from any personal experience.

Polyurethane and such finishes do not really appeal, most carvings do not require a high gloss finish. As I've said, the only works which benefit from such are those tending towards the 'abstract'. Even those are better with a traditional French-polished finish.

Fig. 1

CHIPCARVING

For our first exercise let us try our hand at 'Chipcarving'. The technique is simple and can be applied as decoration to panels or rails for the more robust type of furniture.

Another advantage is the small number of tools required.

This type of decoration is ancient and is found throughout history, occurring in many parts of the world from many diverse cultures.

To mention just a few we find examples in Iceland, Scandinavia, Africa, Italy and Southern Spain.

In Switzerland it is used to good effect on cupboards and other articles in domestic use.

Possibly the best examples of chipcarving design as applied to functional things are the Dutch mangle-boards of the late 18th century. These were used to assist with the wringing out of water from clothes etc. when the laundering was done.

The islands of the Pacific yield examples of chipcarving of great beauty. The Polynesian cultures have throughout history produced articles of use with just the right amount of decoration, neither too much nor too little. One outstanding example is the blade of a paddle for a canoe or similar craft.

The decoration is of necessity shallow cut, but the effect is just right. This particular example is not ancient, being either 18th or 19th century.

In Britain, some of the older churches have chests in which various parish goods, ornamental metal-work and other treasures were kept. The early examples date from the 13th century and are of very simple construction.

Boards of great width were assembled using large nails of wrought-iron. The ends of the chest were generally of thicker material to assist this method of construction.

The wide boards also made available to the carver a large front area for decoration. One example from the late 13th century is at Earl Stonham in Suffolk, not far from Stowmarket. The front has four roundels, each one different. This front is, or appears to be, made of three boards. Made from

Project: A Decorative Motif

Fig. 1. 'Chipcarving' – An ancient method of carved decoration, simple in technique and requiring only a small number of tools.

25

Figs 2 & 3. The chest at All Saints Church, Hereford. Above, the front elevation shows chipcarving development towards Medieval Tracery. The illustration right is of a small detail much enlarged. The work is 13th century.

oak, the outer two are used with vertical grain, the central one having horizontal grain.

Hereford's Church of All Saints has an example also dating from the 13th century. In this example the construction appears to be more advanced, using the less wide outer boards, as stiles into which the main front board is housed. It is shown in the illustration above left, with a small section enlarged to show greater detail above.

The decoration to the stiles is chipcarving in two square motifs to each. The parts of this front corresponding to top and bottom rails in a framed-up construction are also decorated by comparatively simple means.

The main front panel, however, though using a kind of chipcarving, shows a development towards ornament more Gothic in style, suggesting tracery. The effect created is beautiful, even the metal lock-plate with its three key-holes is well accommodated within the design.

I trust the illustration conveys this.

Fig. 5 shows a way in which chipcarving can be used as decoration to borders or to the rails of tables, stools and other furniture.

The tools required for the design shown in *fig. 4* are flat chisels, preferably carving tools. The widths ½in and ¾in.

Gouges: No. 3 in section of various widths up to ¾in.

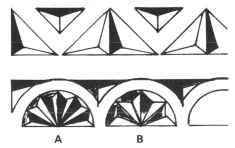

Fig. 4. Layout for a design shows lines to be 'set in'. All the 'pockets' are 'vee' in section and deepest in their centres as indicated here by a broken line.

A   B

Fig. 5. Two suggestions for using chipcarving as decoration to the rails of tables, stools and other furniture. In the lower design, use either arc repeated.

Some carvers use 'whittling knives' for chipcarving. These are much used in America for chipcarving and indeed in many other fields of carving.

Techniques

The various shapes of the 'pockets' are all 'vee' in section and are arrived at by setting in the internal lines only; these are shown as broken lines in the illustration.

These are to be 'set in'; deepest to the centre of each shape.

The sides are then cut as inclined planes meeting on the central lines, the straight sides to the outer triangle pockets are from flat chisels.

The curved sides result from the use of the No. 3 gouges.

Japanese Oak is very pleasant to cut and would suit this exercise.

You will find that with practice this method of decoration can be developed to fit any shape to be decorated. Just as long as the shapes you devise are thought of with the method of cutting in mind — the overall pattern need not be strictly geometric.

Some work in precious metals, also from many ancient cultures, appears to be based on chipcarving, though the technique used may differ.

This could be a field for study in search of designs to carve.

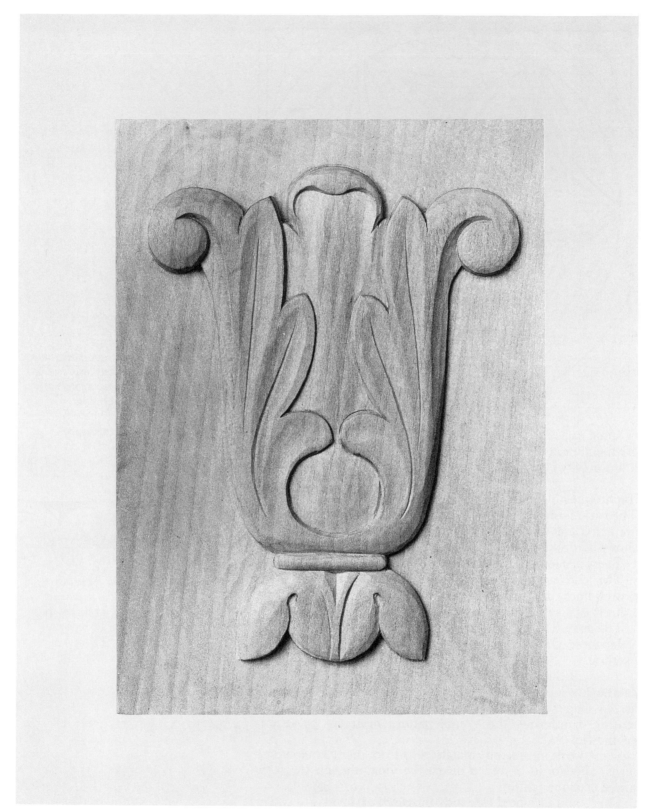

Fig. 1

CARVING IN RELIEF

For our second exercise I have chosen a simple 'husk'. This project has always been popular with beginners and provides an ideal introduction to carving in relief. Sections through the design at points A, B and C will help you to visualize the work in progression.

The minimum size of timber 156 × 114mm (6⅛in long × 4½in) wide, not less than ¾in thick, from any suitable material listed under materials on page 10.

Before we commence the actual carving, I should like to clarify certain points. The main thing to realize is that at this stage of experience there are no short cuts. Every aspect of art or craft, like all other trades, has its own fundamental skills and techniques which must be mastered before advanced work can be attempted.

A genius with 'built-in' knowledge and ability is extremely rare. Therefore I suggest that work be done in a sequence of stages, each one under the carver's full control.

Over the many years I have taught adults, one instance comes to memory of a student jumping in at the deep-end and soon floundering. In an evening class a few years ago an adult-student had been looking at illustrations of Assyrian sculpture in relief. One of the hunting or battle scenes in stone which they did so well and which are milestones in the history of sculpture. The student had commenced his version before attending class. The result was chaotic and resulted in his disillusionment. Fortunately we were able to overcome this in later lessons and the last work of his I saw was very good.

Outline

However, to work. Having the design and suitable material to hand the first thing is to transfer the design to the wood.

Fix the drawing on to your timber and slip a piece of carbon paper between, and go over all the lines of the design with a hard pencil. If the design is secured at the top you can lift the design and carbon to check what has happened. Should any lines be missing, lower the design and go over them.

Project: A Simple Husk

Fig. 1. A simple 'husk', shown here carved in Lime, provides an ideal subject for a beginner in relief carving.

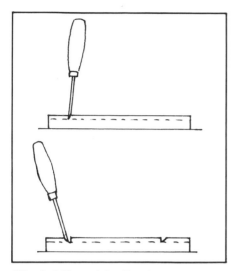

Fig. 2. (Above.) Incline the tool slightly away from the subject when 'setting in' around its perimeter. (Below.) Establishing the outline.

Fig. 3. Below: Note the hand position for maximum control over the gouge when using a mallet. Fig. 4 shows correct position for both hands when using hand pressure only.

Depth Line: Using your fingers as a gauge, run a line around all edges and ends of the wood 6mm (¼in) from the design face. The depth of relief can always be increased later if necessary.

Fasten the wood securely to your bench with a 'G' clamp or 'Holdfast', remembering to use a wastewood block between cramp and subject. Try a No. 3 or 4 gouge against the outline drawn and if it fits begin to set in. It is advisable to incline the tool slightly away from the subject — see *fig. 2*. Continue this process using the tools with section curve appropriate to the outline.

At this stage use a mallet (hand-pressure is insufficient) and go round the outer-line of the subject; the 'coastline' if that idea helps. The lines within this are dealt with later. The design in progress has some long slow curves to each side. Such lines can be cut with a vee parting-tool. Provided that the tool is sharp, held firmly and driven along the line by mallet blows, the result will be better than if set-in. The remainder of the design perimeter is dealt with as already indicated.

This stage being completed, refer to *fig. 2* and establish the outer line by removing a small amount of wood on the waste side of the line. This clarifies the subject's outer shape and can obviate mistakes later. Lines from the vee-tool will already be defined.

Relief

We have now to commence the process of lowering the background to allow our subject to stand in 'Relief'.

This should be done with care and in such a way that the process is under control. Do not attempt to reach the depth line at one fell swoop. Use a five or six gouge.

Place the cutting edge against the end grain of your timber, make this quite a deliberate action until you have had more experience. No 'dive-bomber' techniques, take your time. Tap the tool with your mallet, driving the cutting edge until it meets the setting in where the chips should come away. If it does not, go over the setting in line until it does. The outline will require constant re-setting in as each layer of background is removed.

The work should now give the 'ploughed field' effect shown in *fig. 6*.

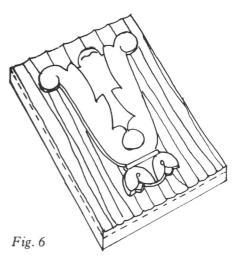

Fig. 6

Fig. 5. Showing sections through the carving superimposed at points 'A' 'B' and 'C' in the horizontal plane, and 'D' in the vertical plane.

Fig. 6. Here the design for the 'husk' has been drawn on the wood surface. Setting in has been completed and taking down the background is in progress.

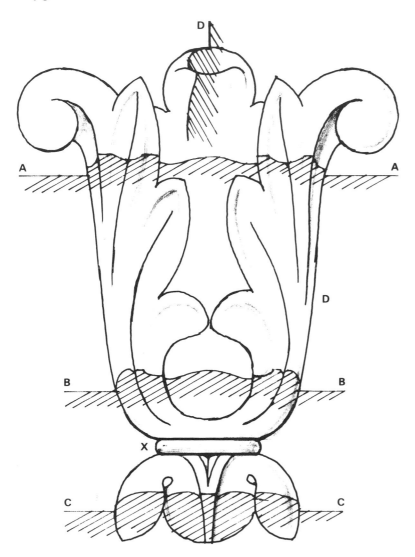

31

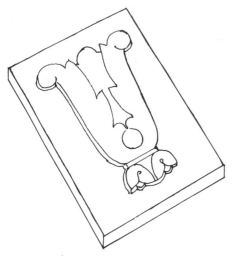

Fig. 7. Shows background removed to depth indicated by broken line seen in fig. 6.

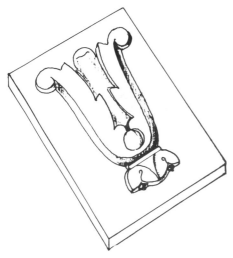

Fig. 8. At this stage, the actual carving of the 'husk' can begin.

Fig. 9. (Opposite) Another example of a decorative 'husk' (carving instructions follow.)

The tops of the ridges are next for removal and these stages are repeated until the depth-line is just showing.

At this stage begin to use a flatter gouge, No. 3 or 4, and gradually complete the background as on the illustration.

The object is not to compete with a plane or router arriving at a flat but dull background surface. The use of your flatter gouges will, if you allow it, give a much livelier surface finish of small facets.

Serrations

When you are satisfied with the background begin to deal with the lines of the leaf serrations within the design. Choose the appropriate tools and set in these lines, not too deep at first. Remove some of the material nearest to the lines; this will indicate that the centre leaf passes under the serrations of the outer leaves.

Do not set in the central lines to these.

If you refer to the sections indicated in the illustration this should help you to visualize the forms to be developed.

'D', for example, shows the leaf tip curling over, so set in the line by hand pressure. The volutes at points 'A' also require the same treatment. The line almost parallel to each side is not set in, but is the result of a hollow plane travelling from 'D' upwards and ending on the set-in volute line. Use a No. 5 to do this, keeping an eye on the section at 'A'.

From 'D' to the collar the hollow form changes to a full curve, 'B'. Take the centre leaf down slightly in height leaving a fullness down the central area, continuing these stages until the desired result is achieved.

Set in the collar lines and work this as a half-round section 'X'. The central vein below this is set in and worked to section 'C'.

Referring to the photograph you will note the slight dishing effect to the surface of the foliage. Use a gouge of medium curve-section and try working these. The central vein is cut with a parting tool.

It does help to think of the growth action of such leaves and to use your tools on the subject with this in mind.

Remember when finishing off, the slow curve gouges — i.e. the shallow ones — can be used with the inside face to the timber surface.

This may help; try it and if you are not too sure about it use the tool in the normal manner. Do not be afraid to experiment in this way on a spare piece of wood. Any such trial will perhaps help to expand your carving technique. The carving can be finished with wax polish and plenty of rubbing with a duster.

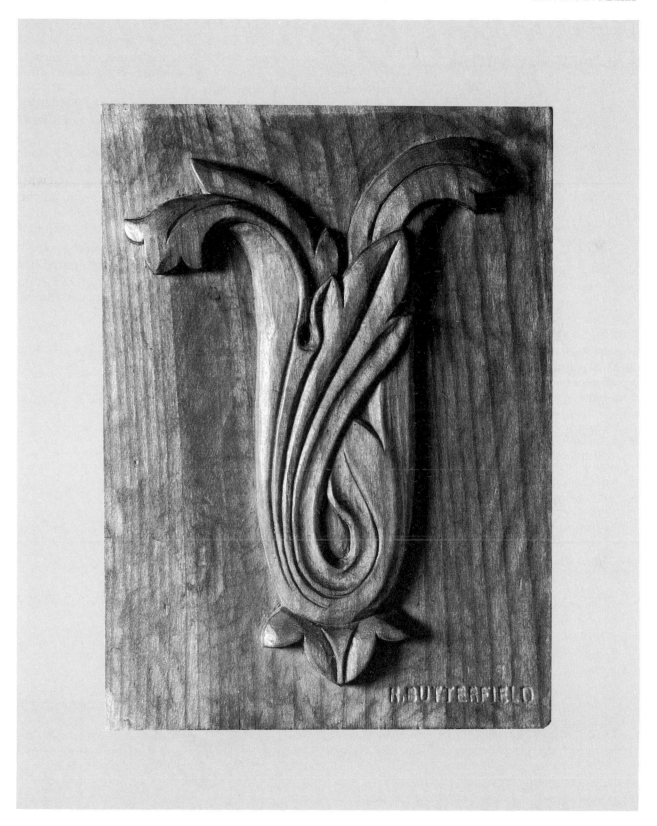

Project: A More Decorative Husk

Our second attempt at 'Relief' carving is another example of a decorative 'husk'. This example is a little more elaborate than the first, showing more alignment with natural form. Choose any suitable wood from those mentioned in the materials list.

Lime if you can obtain it will be the easiest to carve, or one of the Mahogany species, Brazilian perhaps but not Cuban yet.

Japanese Oak may be used, but oak really requires a more robust design for best results. Timber size, not less than 147mm × 115mm (5¾in by 4½in) wide and a minimum thickness of 18mm (¾in).

Notes on Scaling

It is seldom possible to publish a design full size on the page of a book. Furthermore, so far as sizes are concerned, individual requirements can vary. The important thing is that proportions are maintained when scaling both up and down.

Fig. 10. How to scale up the idea and keep it in proportion. Below, the design is placed within ¼in squares each one being numbered. Right: the design on a grid of ½in squares has been enlarged to twice the original size. By registering points on the design in relation to the grid enlargement, the proportions can be checked. For example; just below 8 on the left-hand vertical the outer leaf top begins – and so on.

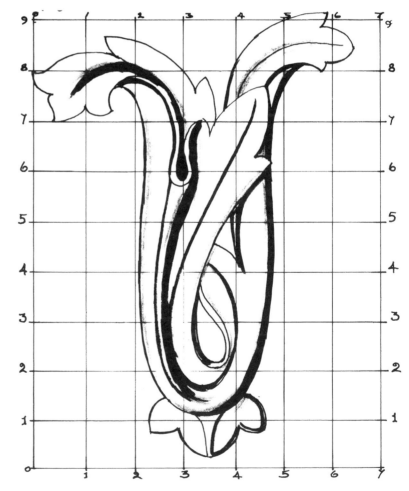

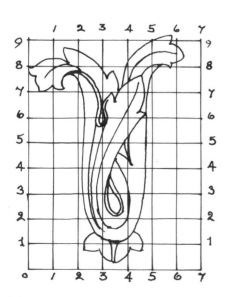

34

Those with access to the latest types of photocopying machines, which are able to variably enlarge and reduce copy, might find it convenient to let a machine do the work. But for most of us scaling up, or down, from the published graph should prove perfectly adequate. The accompanying illustration shows the use of that method in enlarging design ideas to the size you require.

In this instance the overall height of the actual carved portion, not including background, is 118mm ($4\frac{5}{8}$in) and in the illustration is the result of enlarging the small 'idea' to twice its drawn size.

The written description on the drawing should help, but to clarify things I will try to explain the method. This can be used for any enlarging or reducing problem you may have to deal with.

Place the 'idea' within a graph of squares, the size in this instance $\frac{1}{4}$in × $\frac{1}{4}$in each square. Number each square from 0 at the bottom left-hand corner outwards along the base line, then deal with the left-hand vertical line in a similar manner. For ease of reference, number the remaining top and right-hand side.

Prepare a graph of half-inch squares (2 × $\frac{1}{4}$in) having an identical number of squares. Number these also in a similar way. Use tracing paper, the reason will become apparent later.

By referring to the 'idea' graph and transposing each reference point to the larger graph we can scale-up the original idea by two. V = Vertical, A = Across.

At position 8, A on 0, V we find the beginning of an upper curve to the left-hand leaf. Mark this with a pencil.

Follow this curve along passing through V.1 about $\frac{1}{3}$ of the portion of this between 8 and 9 across and by following the sweep already in motion at this point, allow it to progress almost to 8A, 2V. A short diagonal curved line to pass through 3V. 8 across and continue this curve a short way. Draw in the small serration occurring in square 7-8 Across, 2-3 Vertical. Returning to the left-hand vertical 0 to 9 try to draw in the curves to the leaf-end within square 0.1V 8-7 Across.

Add the small inner curve to this leaf-end, and by drawing the inverted 'U' shape 7A between V1&2 the top of the left-hand outer curve of the subject will be determined.

This ends in square 2-3A: 1-2V, and if you mark a point on 3V slightly above 1A and another on line 2A, you should be able to bring the left-hand outer slow curve in a tighter curve for the husk base.

Along 5 Across just before Vertical 5 mark a point and try to draw the descending curve to the curve of the base. Try to draw in the right-hand slow curve, the outer one, relating it to the graph positions and ending through 5V and 8 Across at the top.

Return to the base and by cross referencing each point draw

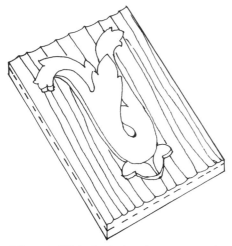

Fig. 11. With the design drawn on, and set-in, the backing is shown in the process of being taken down.

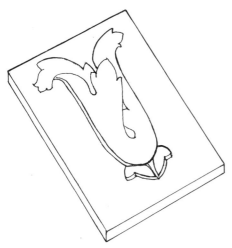

Fig. 12. This shows the background removed down to the depth indicated by a broken line in the top illustration.

in the Trefoil-shaped base to the design. Put in the central vein to this as indicated. Deal with the leaf-shapes within the design by noting on the larger graph positions relative to those on the smaller and you should be able to complete the scaling-up. This method may be a little daunting at first but you will, I am sure, soon get used to it.

A study of the illustration will help more than any attempt to describe the process further by words.

Spacing the design in relation to the wood

For preference I use tracing paper as already mentioned for the scaled-up design; this allows its relationship to timber to be easily seen.

Regarding the positioning of the design on the wood to be used. The side margins should be or perhaps it would be better to say, *appear* to be equal.

The design in question is not exactly balanced on either side of a centre-line. In such cases the *weight of space* must be considered. This means, try the design against the upper face of the wood, move it across this to the position you consider 'optically correct'. In other words place it where it looks right to you.

This process is not something which can be measured with a rule, and will occur throughout all 'relief' carvings. It is a matter of training the eye to see what will result in the best visual effect.

Top and bottom margins

It is always better to have a slightly larger margin at the bottom. Any design, be it a picture within a mount, a paper margin or a carving in relation to its background, if placed exactly central vertically, leaving identical margin size top and bottom, gives the appearance of having slipped. So remember to counteract this by allowing a little extra depth to bottom margins.

There may be many such instances where the 'compensation' is required. They cannot be measured but the need for these will become obvious as your experience grows.

When design has been transferred to timber, put a depth-line around all sides and ends of the material.

Setting in

As in the first project there are lines which can be better arrived at by using a 'Parting Tool', the vee-section tool. Using this will help with the long slow curves at each outer side of the design.

When the remaining perimeter lines are set-in, remove a little wood on the waste side of these, only a little. This helps to establish and make clear the design out-line.

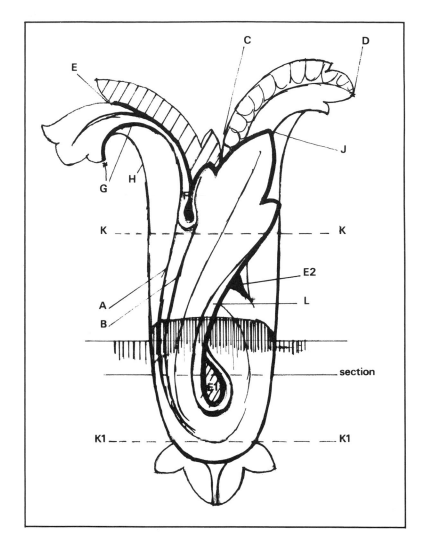

Fig. 13. Progressive sequence for shaping the relief. Before centre veins or other details are put in, look at the shaded section and try to arrive at the shape between broken line K. . . .K and broken line K1. . . .K1. Darker lines should be pressed in by hand deeper at the top and less deep as they travel down.

Removal of background

For this next stage, use a quick gouge at first, say, a number 6 section.

After the 'ploughed field' effect resulting from this, use shallower gouges 3 and 4 to finish off the background at depth-line level. Leave a tooled finish as suggested in the earlier exercise using various widths of No.3 the shallowest gouge. Keep setting in the lines of the design to allow this to have a clean edge and stand out from the background clearly.

Do not tilt setting-in tools away from the subject; this results in undercutting and eventual loss of wood needed in the finishing stages. Also I should like to remind you not to remove too large a quantity at once when lowering the backgrounds. The progression drawing should help to show these stages.

This accomplished we can now tackle the more interesting task of shaping the relief of our subject. *Fig. 13*, the darker

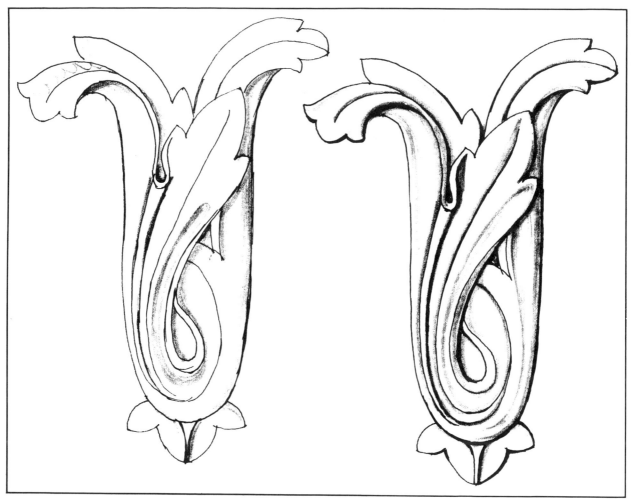

Fig. 14 (Above left). A later stage in the progression of the carving shows actual treatment of the surface with the tops of the outer leaves beginning to curve over. Fig. 15 (Above right) is an impression of how the finished carving should appear.

lines (I trust these will show) indicate lines to be pressed in not too deep, by hand. Lines A and B can be cut in lightly using a parting tool, deeper at the top becoming less deep as they travel down. If on reaching the quicker curve at the bottom you find this tool awkward in negotiating this, set in that portion with the appropriate tools.

Area C-D at the upper part of the right-hand leaf above the centre-line is an inclined plane. The centre-line itself is not as yet set in, but is used as a starting place for the slightly inclined plane.

I shall be using the 'plane' often in the course of this book, so a definition seems appropriate.

A *plane* is a *surface*, it may be *flat, inclined, convex* or *concave*. These are the means by which a carver interprets the subject in hand. Planes are dealt with in greater detail when carving the head of a horse beginning on page 105.

In sculpture the action of light and shade on these surfaces expresses the 'idea'.

Continue with area C-D on *fig. 13*, an inclined plane.

The area E-F indicated by diagonal shading is of a lower general level being farther away from the viewer. Take this area down $\frac{1}{16}$in to give a flat surface allowing the outer, more distant, curving leaf to stand at block surface level for the present. Press in along line 'G', some of this line is already well established as part of the outline, but where it crosses line 'H' press in firmly, lessening pressure as the line travels to area 'F'. Again just remove enough below the arc made to stress its position.

Fig. 14 shows the main area shaded to indicate surface modelling.

Line J of the overlying leaf should show as a darker line mentioned earlier and should be pressed in, or even tapped in gently, with mallet and appropriate tools.

Remove a very small amount from the area to the right of this, i.e. towards the outline. Our object is to make this over-lying leaf appear to do just that.

Line J has an almost parallel line along most of its lower length and running around area E1. Leave this margin at block surface height for now.

The lines bordering the two small areas E1 and E2 should now have been pressed in and these areas can be lowered by almost $\frac{1}{8}$in from the block surface. Try to clean the bottoms of these areas with the aid of a small 'grounding tool'.

If you have small tools, press in lightly the loop effect at F, lower the very small part within the loop as shown on the drawing.

Fig. 13 shows the next development.

Before centre veins or other details are put in, look at the shaded section and try to arrive at this shape between broken line K --- K and broken line K1 --- K1, continuing the rounding process to include the curve of the heavy line at husk base above the final trefoil.

Fig. 14 shows progression in the actual treatment of the surface, with the tops of the outer leaves beginning to curve over, left hand rather more.

A hollow 'flute' running up inside the right hand of the leaf (which overlaps, travels round the bottom E1 position, travelling round the small foil of the right hand leaf) to enhance the effect that this disappears under the overlying leaf.

Fig. 15 shows completion, with the diminishing tunnel-like shape between line A and B *fig. 13* having been rounded along its narrowing progress to what is perhaps best described as a tunnel shape.

The centre veins to the leaves are put in with a parting-tool, if you have one, or set in on the centre lines and a slight Vee shaped channel arrived at. The whole work is then gone over with *fig. 9* in view to be referred to, and the work brought to completion.

Fig. 1. The completed carving of a North American Bison or as it is often called by its local name 'Buffalo'.

CARVING IN RELIEF

For this exercise we leave the field of decorative ornament and attempt to depict a Bison. There are two living species of this animal, the European and the North American, the latter sometimes called by its local name of Buffalo.

Our subject is the American type which for me is far more interesting, conveying the impression, by means of its formidable shoulders and mane, of power and strength.

The object of this exercise is not to produce a photographic representation of the beast but, by using the process of selection and formalisation mentioned earlier, to express the robust strength of the animal.

Material

Japanese Oak will do fine; other suitable timbers may be found listed under materials.

With the grain running along the largest dimension, the size required is 203mm (8in) long by a minimum of 145mm (5¾in). Ex 25mm (1in) in thickness or better still Ex 32mm (1¼in) which finishes around 28mm (1⅛in) thick after planing.

Leave a strip of the material half an inch from the bottom edge, the full thickness of the wood. Our subject stands on this as is shown in the design.

Draw the subject on the face of the wood, square the baseline on to the ends and run a depth-line around the sides and top 9mm (⅜in) deep from the face side. The object being to remind you to leave the bottom strip at full thickness; all carving is to be above this line.

Setting in

Secure the timber to the bench top by a G-cramp with a packing piece (or use a holdfast if you have one), again using some packing between this and the wood being carved. Select tools with section-shapes to fit the outline and start to set in the outside line only.

Project: A Bison

Fig. 2. The design full-size can be traced and then transferred to the wood. Ensure that a half-inch strip at full thickness is left at the base for the subject to stand on.

That is, along the forward base-line up to the front hoof.

From here, up the leg and continuing along the neck, around the beard and head arriving at the shoulders which are the highest point. From this position continue down the back, then the outer-line of the tail, down the leg to base-line and cut along this to the outer edge of the wood. Remember, a slight buttress effect to edges helps.

Leave the three spaces between the legs for the present and, using a No. 6 or similar gouge ⅜in or ½in wide, begin the process of taking down the background area.

If the wood proves awkward to cut one way, turn the block around and try from the other direction.

If before beginning this process you remove a small amount of wood on the waste side up to the setting-in lines, this will establish the actual design and help to prevent encroachment on this when removing the background.

The use of the No. 6 gouge up to and stopping on the outline will give the background surface the 'ploughed field' effect. Keep on setting-in and removing the background a layer at a time until you are almost at the depth-line. At this stage change to a shallow gouge and complete the background with a tooled surface.

Whilst using the No. 6 gouge you will find it better not to try to continue each groove its entire length at one go. It helps to cut so far, then withdraw the gouge and continue the grooves in stages.

The three spaces between the legs may now be dealt with, remembering the slight incline away from those parts to be left standing; do not undercut.

When the lines concerned, including that along the base, have been set in remove a small portion of wood on the waste side of each to establish the leg and hoof shapes; also the underside of the body in the central space.

The removal of the wood between the legs to background level should be done with care using Nos. 5 or 6 section, then once more finish with the shallower Nos. 3 or 4.

The space around the tail is also removed by this process but do it with care a little at a time; do not rush such tasks.

Interpretation

In Relief the subject is generally dealt with in profile. Three-quarter and front views are very difficult to translate satisfactorily into relief.

Our main concern is to translate the idea of our subject, a freestanding animal, into something which can be carved in half an inch or less of relief. This means that all form is interpreted with a degree of flatness. A good example of such treatment is the head on coinage.

Perhaps the best way to deal with the problem is to view the design and decide on those parts which are nearest to us. These will be the highest points of relief, whilst those farthest away will appear as the lowest.

With this in mind, lower the height of the legs and hooves on the far side of the body. Set-in the line of the chest across the forward leg and that which crosses the forward of the two rear-legs.

Continue from here along the line which separates the nearer hind leg from its partner, setting in at a lesser depth where it passes for a short distance over the flank of the animal. These lines should not be set-in too deeply; hand-pressure will do but if this is difficult for you, tap them in lightly with a mallet.

Take enough from the surface of these legs to lower their upstand from the background to about one eighth of an inch.

The end of the tail can now be set-in where this passes over the rear-most hind limb; again press these lines in lightly. Treat the beginning of the tail in a similar way but remember that the tail would spring from the centre-line of the back if viewed in plan.

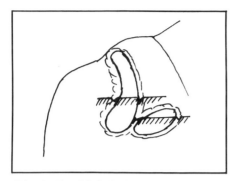

Fig. 3. Establish the horn and ear shape. The horn is the highest relief on the head. The ear is in slightly less relief.

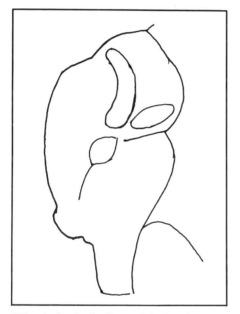

Fig. 4. Set in the lines of the head, including the outer-line of the eye only. These lines should still be showing after the surface has been lowered, thus saving the need to re-draw.

To show this in relief we must lower the surface of the tail slightly, allowing the line of the lower back to continue past and on down the hind leg.

Remove a small amount from the tail surface at this point and look at the effect produced; if this appears to suggest that the tail is as mentioned above, leave that part for the present and deal with the end of the tail.

By removing a little wood from the surrounding surface up to the setting-in lines of the tail we shall arrive at the effect required, i.e. that the tail does pass over the rear limb.

Looking at the subject as suggested, the shoulders and the vertical left fore-leg are the areas nearest to the viewer and the highest part of the relief.

The Head

This is generally slightly lower in relief, but the horn and ear are slightly nearer to the viewer.

Set-in the outline of these and remove a small amount of wood. Remember always to incline the tool in use to produce the buttress effect; the slight slope is always from that part to be shown in highest relief. This is shown in *fig. 3* and establishes the horn and ear shapes.

Continuing in the area of the head, set in the two curves behind the head, then the outer line of the eye, showing the slow curve from the corner of this. Do not set in the muzzle lines yet.

This done, remove with shallow gouges, i.e. Nos. 3 or 4 in section, about one eighth of an inch from the surface of this area, leaving the horn and ear at the full thickness of your wood in order to create the fullness of relief required.

Setting in the eye and other line should leave these showing when the surface has been lowered and so save having to draw them again. If they do tend to become fainter, press them in before removing more wood.

Surface modelling

The curve which shows the forward thrust of the shoulder mass behind the head, and terminating at the top of the foreleg nearest to us, will begin this process. Do not set this in but use a ⅜in No. 6. gouge or the tool you have nearest to this size and section. Carve a more shallow groove along this line.

Fig. 5 shows a curved groove at the rear of the shoulder mass, carve this slightly deeper with the same gouge.

Continuing from the lower end of this, set-in the rear lines of the left fore-leg and take a little wood away from the rear of this to indicate that eventually the lower outline of the body passes between the front legs.

If the front line of this leg is also set in where it crosses the chest, and similar amount of wood removed, this will help that effect.

Figs 5 & 6 show work in progress and the next stage of dealing with the general levels of relief.

Extend the curve of the hind leg nearest to you so that it passes for a short way across the flank. This line will be deepest where the body passes between the rear-legs, becoming less so as it proceeds. Remove a little wood on the flank side of this.

Progression
The progression drawing will show the next stage, which is to deal with the general levels of relief. The horn, ear, shoulder mass and left fore-leg are the highest relief at this stage whilst the parts in deeper tone are progressively lower in relief.

Head and Shoulders
Returning to this area, press in again the two curves at the back of the head and, working with a ⅜in shallow gouge, on the surface between the forward shoulder thrust line and the set in lines at the rear of the head.

Carve an inclined plane towards these, giving a suggestion of a neck before the weighty shoulders. Shape the back of the head as shown in *fig. 4*, leaving a small vertical edge to the forms.

It is a good thing to remember not to fade relief, either into the background or to allow forms within the general outline to fade into those surrounding.

If this is done, the effect may be subtle but never shows any apparent fullness of form. For example, the lines behind the head should be left with a little vertical upstand otherwise the head fades into the neck without any poll or jaw-line.

The horn, as said earlier, is the highest relief on the head. Keeping in mind the flatness of treatment advised, begin to shape this. The ear is in slightly less relief.

The horn is actually circular in section but do not attempt to depict this as semi-circular in relief; a stronger effect is gained by only slightly rounding the outside edges.

Tuck the poll in a little in front of the horns to suggest that it passes between them. The mass of this part of the hair extends down the front to reach the nose. This latter is however a different shape and form and should be interpreted as such.

The ear has a slight hollow within its borders and this should be carved with a small No. 5 or 6 gouge. The poll should be dealt with again to show that it is lower around the ear; also the cheek lowered slightly at this position.

The eye outer-line is already set-in; make two small vee curves by cutting to the outside of these lines.

With a small gouge, set-in the edges of the eye-lids and try to suggest the form of the eye within. Do this carefully and keep observing the effect produced. Do not pursue too far and when you feel satisfied, leave it. Too much striving with such details can result in the removal of wood better left.

One thing should be kept in mind when carving an eye, either in the 'round' or in 'relief', and that is the working of the eyelids. These should give the impression that they could close; too many eyes are depicted with lids which are merely lines. Do try to give them some degree of substance and if you are in any doubt get a mirror and look at your own.

Front Legs

Dealing with the one in lowest relief, set in the bottom edge of the hair which cloaks much of the forelegs.

Remove a little wood from the surface of the leg and hoof where these protrude from the hair, and begin to shape these as the photograph shows.

Remember the hooves are cloven so indicate by a slight groove on the front of each with a small quick gouge. Try to indicate the fringe of the hair at the back lower surfaces as shown, not by attempting to show each hair but rather by the grouping of locks and indicating these by small set-in curves from various tools. Cut these as shown to lines of vee-section.

Hindquarters

These are by contrast much lighter. Work over the surface of these and reduce the general height of relief a little before attempting any detail. The chest is carved to show that the planes of this pass under the lower shoulder mass rear line.

The left hind-leg stands a little higher and the body is lowered to pass between this and its partner.

Finish shaping the tail and rear hooves.

The left leg has a tendon behind the lower portion running down to the hoof. Show this by a slight hollow below the bony angle of the joint.

Compare your work with *fig. 2* and continue working with this before you. Try for a simplicity of interpretation.

CARVING IN THE ROUND

Project: A Bear

Fig. 1. The Bear carved in Brazilian Mahogany. The idea offers scope for being carved as a money box.

I n this exercise the subject is carving in the 'round'. The term 'in the round' means a free-standing carving, viewable from all sides. For a first attempt at this type of work a robust, chunky subject is better than attempting to deal with finer details of limbs.

'The Bear' is designed with this in mind. Some years ago I was asked to carve an animal-shaped money box; the subject could form the basis for such a project. One thing to remember is that if this is to be the aim of the exercise, the hollowing out of the interior and the insertion of a coin-slot in the top of the head will have to be dealt with.

Therefore no surface carving should be too deeply cut or we shall have holes appearing.

Material

Brazilian mahogany is easy to get at presen' carves well and has a good colour. The carved example will be in this wood.

Thickness: this is the most important measurement because to a great degree it decides the size that anything can be carved. I suggest a minimum thickness of 80mm (3⅛in), width 87mm (3⅜in), with a height including the base. The actual height of the bear itself has workd out at 159mm (6¼in) high on the carved example.

Draw the profile of the bear on each of the larger sides. It is best to draw on one side then square salient points across the thickness and measure into the outline at these points to position the drawing on the other side.

If the subject is drawn on tracing paper this will help you to see the wood for positioning. These squaring points would be the base line, leaving material below this to hold work in the vice and for possible future use as a base:

The tip of the muzzle and the distance in along the base up to the paw at the front and up to the back of the animal at the rear.

Other points can be used should you feel them necessary. Check that the two profiles do indeed tally.

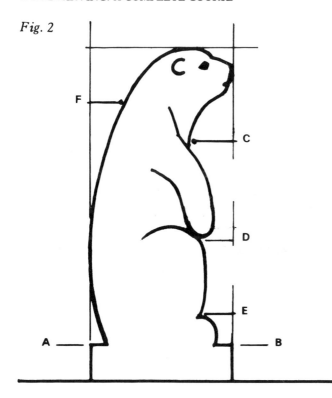

Fig. 2

Fig. 3

Fig. 2. Saw cuts indicated on this illustration go squarely through the block. A and B are saw-cuts to show the base.

Side view saw cuts and roughing out

Saw cuts should now be made as indicated in *fig. 2*, remembering that these go squarely through the block linking both sides.

Place the timber in the vice face down, using some packing to the vice-jaws if necessary. Secure the wood in this position and begin to remove areas 'A' shown in *fig. 3*. A fairly large gouge should be used, a number 7 section shape, ¾in wide.

When you are approaching the outline put down this deep gouge and complete this part using a number 3 or 4 of similar width or smaller.

Using this, work until the outline is reached. These shallower section tools will be of particular assistance when carrying the outline of the lower back down to the base line; a deeper section tool will mark the base.

Turn the wood over so that the front is uppermost.

Draw a pencil line square across the wood where the underside of the chin commences. Using the same tools, start to remove the mass from this starting line with diagonal cuts towards the saw cut as in *fig. 4*. This should clear the chippings at that point.

Should you find it difficult to carve near to the actual line from chin to the top of the fore-legs, leave a margin and come back to that part later. By cutting towards C and D in the directions shown by the hatching in *fig. 4* the bulk of waste will be removed.

Fig. 4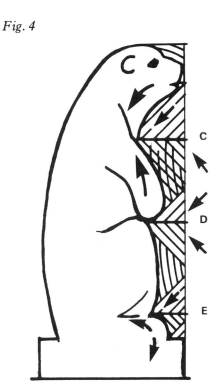

Fig. 5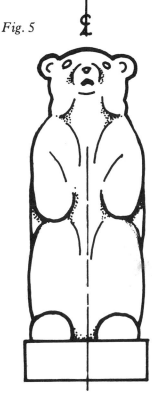

Fig. 6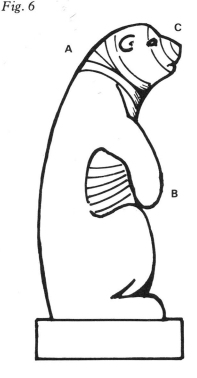

Now move on to the part between D and E and remove excess timber in a similar way, always cutting away the triangular shape towards each successive saw-cut first. This 'opens the door' to allow for tools to take the centre portion down to the outline. A smaller width 6 or 7 section will be better here, say one ⅝in wide, continuing the use of a 3 or 4 when approaching the outline.

Finally take out the portion between E and the base line.

This should give a complete side view when the small portions remaining in the facial area are dealt with.

If the neck line above C has proved difficult try persuading the wood to cut by cutting diagonally across the grain or even straight across. So long as you only remove a little at a time this should solve the problem.

Development of form
Draw a centre line on the front of the wood, up from the base line and continuing over the top of the head, down the back to reach the base line at the rear of the animal.

The small sketch of the front view in *fig. 5* will give a basic idea of the ultimate shape.

The head is less wide than the body and the measurement across from ear to ear will be the widest part of the head. The narrowest will be the muzzle and snout.

By now you should have some idea as to which way the grain runs in the wood being used. Working in the appropriate

Fig. 5. This front view gives a basic idea of the ultimate shape.

Fig. 7

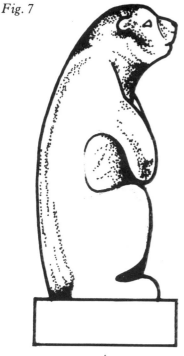

Fig. 8

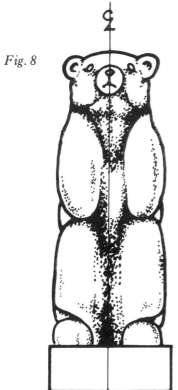

Figs 7 & 8 show the work more advanced. The masses of the ears are set in and left standing.

direction, remove a little wood from the surface at the places indicated by the shading on *fig. 6*.

Use a ⅜in wide No. 4 or 5 section gouge and at 'A' carve a slightly concave plane. The plane will be carried under the head and should not be deep, only sufficient to indicate the neck area.

'B' is a shallow depression from under the fore-limb, down and bordering the top of the knee, sloping away slightly from the highest part at the back. These areas are not set-in, the borders of each portion are arrived by the use of the gouge, giving a dish-like effect.

Deal with the corresponding areas on the other side of the Bear.

Figs. 7 and *8* show the work more advanced. The masses of the ears are set-in and left standing as the surrounding parts of the head are reduced in level to the shapes indicated.

The line of the jowl or cheek is left high with the head shaping carried on in front and the neck shaping worked behind.

The paws can now be shaped; this shaping to be kept soft, no claws attempted.

Between the level of the paws, reduce the body slightly by about 6mm (¼in) to arrive at the surface of the 'tummy'.

Carry this shaping down and make a hollow plane, not too deep, between the knees. Remove a small amount at base-level to separate the hind feet and allow the hollow plane above to run down into this.

Remember the problem of hollowing if it is to be used for a money-box; as mentioned earlier, do not cut too deeply into the surfaces.

The hind feet can be indicated by a cut along the top of these and small amounts of wood being removed above this — i.e. a slightly inclined plane as indicated in *figs. 7* and *8*.

The vertical front of these legs should now be dealt with by carving them with a rounded surface, full on the vertical but less so at the knee.

Here, a slightly inclined plane from the top to where the leg joins the body at the end of a very slow downward curve. Deal with the other rear leg in the same way.

With reference to *fig. 9*, an illustration in pen and wash: 'A' first shows the subject in side view, whilst 'B' is an attempt to show the main planes required to reveal the structure of the head. Should you find this process difficult, study the sketch in front and side views and try searching the wood for these planes.

I can only liken it to exploring, using gouges no deeper than sections 3 and 4 and starting with the profile of the head free from any excess wood, with the snout narrowed as the illustration suggests. Cut the top of the snout with three planes, one slightly rounded on top and one at each side immediately touching, slightly inclined away from this. They are not flat, but as shown are a little curved.

The top of this part is like the temple on a human head; cut this at each side of the head as a slightly hollow surface, highest near the ear, and sweeping across to meet the plane which gives the position of the eye.

Eyes

These planes which are diagonally shaded show, as said above, the position where the eye will be curved.

Try to visualize the eye functioning. It must look as though an upper lid will close over it, and must suggest its ability to move within its socket to look in various directions.

Fig. 10. This is an attempt to convey the head at a stage further advanced and beyond the pen and wash illustrations. Here the form has been refined by the use of smaller planes giving a softer effect.

Details of eyes nose and mouth have been carved and with some further slight softening to the edges of the planes, the head can be completed.

The eyes were carved with a No. 7 section gouge ³/₁₆in wide.

Completion

Once the head and eyes are finished the completion of the body and limbs should be comparatively easy. The diagrams and photograph should help you more than the written word. However, the following notes may assist.

Keep the back of the animal broad, with a soft round shape when viewed from above.

At the base the front vertical shape of the hind legs is slightly wider than at the back, giving a little splay.

The fore-legs are less if measured across the outer-edges of the paws than at shoulder width. The paws are to be kept very simple in shape with no hard edges.

Money-Box

If this is to be the result, it is better to leave the base of the original block on to enable the work to be held secure in the vice.

Turn the work upside down and fasten it in the vice. Check where the bulk of the wood is enough to allow passage of a large diameter drill or bit. Failing this draw a rectangle on the underside of the base well within the bulk.

On the example carved this works out at 38mm (1½in) across the front and back by 38mm (1⅜in) from back to front.

Draw diagonals across the rectangle to find the centre and, at a point 6mm (¼in) along these from each quarter, mark with a centre punch. Drill a hole at each with 6mm (¼in) diameter.

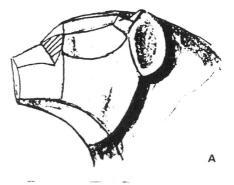

A

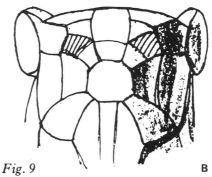

Fig. 9

B

Fig. 10

Fig. 9 A & B. The head: Front and side views showing the 'Planes' arrived at when exploring the structure of this. Fig. 10 shows the head in an advanced stage with the form refined by smaller planes to give a softer effect.

Fig. 11. The carving can be finished with a diluted coat of white shellac to seal the surface and when completely dry, wax polished.

Next use a brace and ¾in bit and in the centre of the rectangle drill a hole. This can be 76mm (3in) deep. The ¼in holes should for safety only be 50mm (2in) deep.

Other smaller diameter holes can be drilled along the sides but within the rectangle.

When as much as is safely possible has been done in this method, the holes can be converted into one cavity by the use of your gouges and the actual sides trimmed with flat chisels.

Base

Remember that a base block will be required unless you wish to leave the holding piece for this. To do this will be quite all right and will give an additional depth to the cavity of the thickness of this base. In this case a sub-base of lesser thickness will be screwed on to close the money box.

Should it be your intention to remove the original base after the hollowing process, remember that any new base will be screwed on. So allow for positioning the screws, leaving sufficient thickness to receive these in the appropriate places.

The new base can be of contrasting colour or material if you wish; remember the grain will be better if it passes across the front of the animal. Let the end grain be on the sides.

Turners may wish to add a turned plinth for a base. I leave that to you.

The coin-slot

This can be made by the drilling method. Draw the slot central between the ears at a point which will not result in the hole perforating the throat area. The slot will pass from such a position and curve along the back slope of the head. The size when finished to be 35mm (1⅜in) long, large enough to take a 50 pence piece.

Drill along the length of the slot inclining the holes slightly inwards from each end. Clear out the slot with chisels making sure that it does enter the cavity. Test it with a coin to be sure when completed.

To polish, brush the surface with diluted white shellac. This will seal the surface and also help if the bear is to be handled a lot.

When completely dry, wax polish applied and given plenty of rubbing with a duster should give a not too treacly finish.

DECORATIVE CARVING

After our venture into working 'in the round' we return to decorative carving in 'relief'. This design is based on Acanthus Foliage, a plant which has often given ideas for decoration in many materials.

There are two botanic types of this plant which grows wild in Southern Europe. Acanthus spinosus and Acanthus mollis, which has broader leaves.

As in all design, nature is used only as a basis. The design could be used as a basic suggestion for decoration on classical style furniture. One idea would be to use it as suggested in *fig. 1*.

With some modification and possibly a little infilling to the lower centre, this could be applied to a pediment or adapted for other layouts of decoration.

Project: An Acanthus Scroll

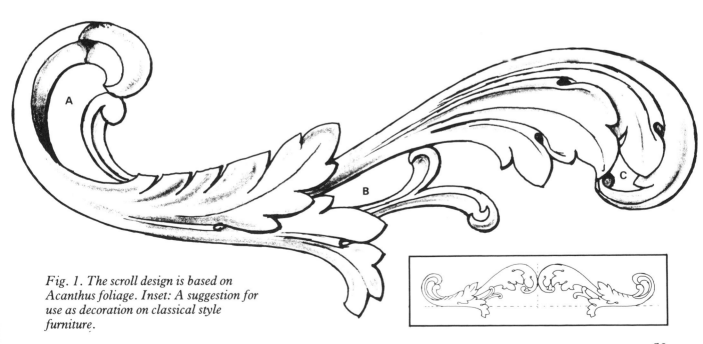

Fig. 1. The scroll design is based on Acanthus foliage. Inset: A suggestion for use as decoration on classical style furniture.

53

Fig. 2. An example carved in sycamore, a hardwood with awkward grain. Lowering the background in progress. This shows the different directions of gouge-cut necessary. Note the difference of approach compared with that required by lime, a more amenable timber.

Material and setting on

Once again, Lime will be the easiest timber to carve but the Brazilian mahogany now available can be used to good effect. Alternatively, make a selection from the list on page 10.

The size: between 200 and 230mm (8in or 9in) long and 100mm (4in) wide, ex 25mm (1in) board thickness from saw.

Transfer the design to the wood by the use of carbon paper, run a depth-line around the sides and ends of your block 9mm (⅜in) deep. This may be slightly deeper than usual but is necessary to gain the full relief effect.

Procedure

As in previous exercises in 'relief', choose the appropriate tools for setting in and sharpen them.

Deal with the perimeter of the design only at present, set this in and remove a small amount of wood on the waste side of the lines to clarify them.

Removal of the excess wood from the background is the next stage. This has been described in previous chapters; remember the 'ploughed field' effect first using a ½in or ⅜in wide gouge No. 6.

Finish off the background at the depth indicated with a No. 3 gouge section of similar width.

Set in the enclosures indicated on the design at 'A', 'B' and the smaller 'C'. Remove a little wood on the waste side within these. Continue to set in and remove wood in these places until a general background level is reached.

Grounding tools

Small size grounding tools will help greatly in the process described above. They are referred to by many names in tool lists and catalogues but basically are cranked chisels.

They may be fish-tailed, i.e. spreading to a width wider than the shank at the cutting edge, or they may be parallel throughout their length.

I have one favourite about ¼in wide at the cutting edge. It is a very old tool and much less weighty than its modern counterpart.

Background

Fig. 2 shows the difference of approach when lowering the background in Sycamore compared to that described when carving Lime.

Sycamore is harder and has grain which often needs a great deal of persuasion from many directions before it will cut cleanly. Some of the texture shows that a diagonal cutting across the grain was necessary in places.

Leave the background at the texture resulting from finishing with shallow No. 3 section gouge.

Interpretation of form

Set the lines of the overlying leaf at position 'A' on *fig. 3*. Remove a little wood on the shaded side to establish in your mind which portion is highest.

The shaded portion indicates an inclined plane; this will eventually be developed to show that this part passes under the upstanding leaf edge.

The effect is similar to the 'Husk' used in a previous exercise. There it was said that this was sometimes used as a springing point for further foliage. The left-hand portion of the present design is just such an example.

The smaller volutes should be lowered in height as at position 'B' in *fig. 3*. This will show that the line of the overlying leaf is dominant.

The upper of the lesser volutes at position 'A' is carved in the manner of the larger one at the left-hand side of the design. The lower differs only in that the volute is foliated to become a curled lead.

The volute on the left of the subject can now be tackled.

As indicated on the design this consists of a hollow cove-like shape on the inside and a full rounded section to the outer edge.

Whilst working in this area, treat the smaller volute within with a similar section.

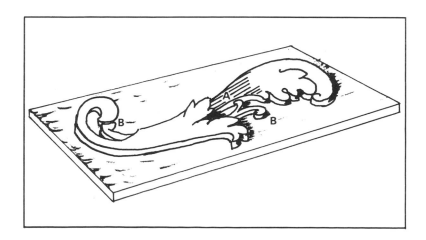

Fig. 3. Background lowered and lines of overlying leaf defined. Note: The smaller volutes have been lowered in height at position B.

Fig. 4. An example of the scroll carved in Lime, a more amenable timber.

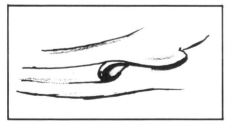

Fig. 5. Details of the eyelet on lower left hand of the design.

The overlying leaf

This, which occupies the left-hand half of the design, has already been set in and its general height established. The actual shaping of the surface has yet to be done.

Carve the detailed outline of the over-lying leaf including the lower edge and remove a small amount of timber below and up to this. Leave the 'eye' or loop where the leaf below is joined. These 'eyelets' are always a problem for students; see *fig. 5* which shows an eyelet in more detail.

The underlying leaf should now appear to do just that and the carving of the detail can be attempted.

Use the gouge you feel is right and begin. The shaping should appear to grow from the centre-vein of the leaf, so draw this in and use a small parting-tool to carve along the line.

Do this lightly for now, too much mallet here will certainly not help, so I stress the word 'lightly'.

From this vein with a small No. 5 or 6 section gouge ¼in wide if you have such, start to explore the form of the leaf. It does help to keep in mind the idea of growth when dealing with such problems; the upper forms, hollows and full shapes grow upwards from the centre-vein and curve over and downwards in the lower part.

The lower underlying leaf

The hollow shapes to each leaf foil radiate from the eyelet, gradually becoming lower in relief and flowing higher towards the termination of the leaf-foils.

Under the eyelet some forms by-pass this and help to form the lower edge of our subject design.

The full rounded shape to the outer edge of the main volute

56

mentioned earlier flows into this lower edge. The foils of the leaf emerge from this in a slightly radiating manner.

With a gouge of medium curved section carve slight hollows along each foil following the radiating curves until these run into the general shaping of the bottom edge on its way towards the volute.

The right-hand leaf

The outer curve of this is full but terminates in a very small volute.

Set in the leaf-foils and with a small No. 5 or 6 section gouge begin to carve the small groove-like shapes to allow the up-standing 'tunnel' forms which extend back from each eyelet.

These are not sudden shapes but grow out of the leaf-foil in front of them. Here again, think of growth flow as you carve; it does help.

The tunnels become narrower as they travel away from the eyelets, finally merging with the other forms.

With the same tools carve the surface of the leaves to the liveliness which I trust is apparent in the photograph of the finished example.

Remember, there is an overlying part to this leaf, so working as before try to make the final right-hand foil appear to pass under its neighbour.

Complete the carving by going over the whole of it, checking shapes and the form. Clean up the background if necessary until you feel satisfied with the whole design.

Polish with wax, not forgetting sides and edges of the background timber.

Fig. 6. An alternative design for an Acanthus Scroll.

57

Fig. 1

FURTHER
CARVING IN RELIEF

Birds of prey have always fascinated me and there have been occasions when this interest has been put to practical use. Many years ago when I was asked to design and carve a series of newel capitals for a house in Warwickshire, two of the subjects used were a peregrine falcon and a long-eared owl.

Other instances have been when an eagle lectern has been commissioned. Ten of these are in churches scattered over a large area, the most distant is in Windsor, Ontario, Canada, and the nearest to my home is in St Matthew's Church, Sheffield. None are carved to a set idea, each one was the result of a re-look at nature.

The design of the tawny owl for this exercise has been drawn to suit material, tools and students' abilities. The object is not 'taxidermy in wood'. The element of design must never be forgotten and some simplification of natural form is always necessary.

To begin

The material used in the carved example is French Walnut. This gives less 'grain trouble' than the English variety.

The size is 180mm × 100mm (7in × 4in), ex 25mm (1in) in thickness. Transfer the design to the face of the wood with carbon-paper and run a depth-line around sides and ends a quarter of an inch deep.

Set in the outer lines only with the appropriately sectioned gouges then begin to lower the background surface as described previously.

Remember in relief carving to look at your design and note the parts which are to be nearest to you the viewer. These will of course be the parts carved in highest relief.

Beak

In the present subject the central portion of the wing will be highest, but we must allow for the projection of the beak from the facial-plane.

Project:
A Tawny Owl

Fig. 1. The finished carving.

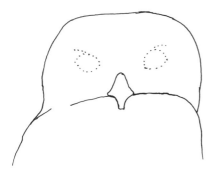

Fig. 2. Set in the beak and wing shoulder line to the right which will be slightly deeper than the remainder.

Fig. 3. Set in the forward edge of the wing and carry on around the lower lines of the wing tips.

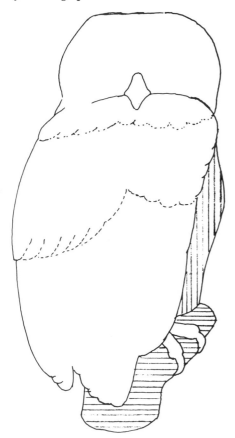

Set in the beak outline and the top of the wing, the shoulder part to the right of the beak will be slightly deeper than the remainder. (See *fig. 2*).

Remove a small amount of wood from the facial area leaving the beak at full thickness of the block. On this new level draw in the eyes, these are shown as dotted lines on *fig. 2*. Press these lines in with hand-pressure only.

Wing

Fig. 3 shows the next step; set in the forward edge of the wing, carrying on around the lower lines of the wing tips. Then the short line denoting the lower edge of the body above the feet and on towards the toes and claws.

When setting in the latter, give the cuts a slight buttress to minimise the danger of breakage.

Lower the horizontal shaded areas of *fig. 3* by 3mm (⅛in) and the bird will be in higher relief than the perch.

The portion of the perch beyond the feet can be a slightly inclined plane, sloping with the lowest level where the branch ends.

Cape of feathers

Owls are a very large family and many of the species have a cape of feathers to the upper back and shoulders. It is this which gives the illusion that the bird turns his head completely. It does not of course, but the cape does add to that impression.

The bottom edge of this can be pressed in lightly indicating the overlay of feathers as in the design. Below this, the next lines indicate the covering feathers to the upper part of the wing, shown as broken lines. They can now be pressed in, again giving some idea of overlay.

The wings curve to the body and with this in mind it would help if, before proceeding further with the feathering details, some attempt was made to convey this curvature.

Fig. 5, area B, denotes the left-hand wing which is just a little farther away from the viewer. Lower this a little and work the outer portion to a curved plane falling away towards the background. Leave at least 2mm or almost ⅛in of vertical edge before reaching the background.

The latter is a good thing to keep in mind in all relief carving, some small amount of almost vertical edge gives the work clarity. Do not let forms disappear into the background unless you have a very good reason for doing so.

The front of the body should also be given a similar rounded effect, the section forward of the wings, although now lower relief should have a fuller curve to the front edge.

The cape and covering feathers should also be given a curve so that this section is now applied to all the bird below the head and beak.

This completed, replace any lines of feathering etc. which may have been lost in the process. Part C on *fig. 4* shows the short feathers there delineated.

Using a parting-tool with its vee-section to cut the straighter parts of the lines, the ends of the feathers make too tight a curve to be dealt with in this manner so set them in with the gouges of appropriately shaped section.

Once lined in, not too deep, an attempt must be made to establish the relative relief of the surfaces.

Flight

In order to get the maximum support during flight, the wing feathers overlie each other to a degree. The leading edge of each slightly overlies the feather in front of it.

However, try to guard against any effect likely to look like steps. Strive to convey the feather arrangements shown in the design without coarseness. The flight of an owl is silent; keep in mind the softness of the feathers and if at first the lines do appear a little harsh this can be subdued later. For the present, concentrate on lowering slightly each feather or part of a feather in sequence. Work over the surface gently inclining it to the effect that part of it appears to pass under its neighbour.

Make sure that all the feathering shown on the design is now established on the carving. The flight feathers have soft-rounded ends, this is another contributor to silent flight.

The head

Returning to this, the eyes should already be pressed in by hand-pressure. They are large and almost round, the line on the top is also pressed in and a very small upstand above this is left.

At the outer corner of each eye press in a short line. Work the surface of the eyeballs round; leave surrounding wood upstanding. Try to achieve the effect that the eyeball is capable of movement within its socket. The circle of feathers surrounding each eye form a very shallow saucer-shape. Tool this gently with gouge of No. 3 section. Perhaps working with the cuts appearing to radiate from the eye outwards towards the saucer rim may help. Try; then view the results. If they appeal to you, carry on. If not, perhaps you are removing too much with each cut. Subdue this.

The beak can be given more shape now, remember it hooks over the wing shoulder. Think of the strength it must have to tear flesh when feeding. Give a strong section shape to the beak as indicated in the design.

Leg and foot

The feet, or foot I should say, as only one shows in the design, the other we must assume to be tucked up into the feathers.

These emerge from under the broad inner wing feathers of

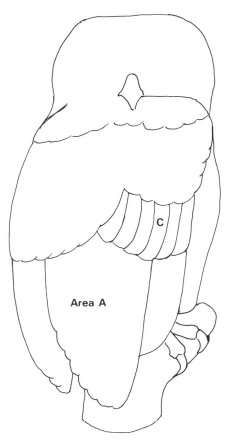

Fig. 4. Area 'C' shows the short feathers delineated. The straight parts of the line can be set-in using a parting-tool with its vee-section. The curved ends of the feathers should be set-in with gouges of appropriately shaped section.

the design. Owls perch with two toes in front and two behind, not in the usual position of three in front and one behind found in the majority of perching birds. Press in the lines of the end of each toe just before the commencement of the claw. Lower the surface of the claw.

The leg itself is within the mass of feathers; the length of leg which actually shows, varies in the different types of owls. A barn owl has a greater length of leg which shows both when in flight or when perching.

Returning to the claws, by reducing the thickness as above, this will help to indicate that the claw is less in thickness than the toe to which it is attached. Try to make the claws look as though they grip the branch on which the bird is resting.

It may be that you feel a need for more working height to the subject as it develops, if so re-set in the perimeter of the design and lower the background a little. First running a new depth-line around the edges and ends to work to. You may find the extra depth gives more scope when the feathering of the wings is in progress.

In designs such as this you will find that the work itself will suggest any need for greater depth, there is nothing arbitrary above the first depth given.

Completion
The softening of the feather surfaces and the lines of the edges of these can be achieved by using a No. 3 section gouge at about ⅜in wide. Work on each feather or that portion of each which shows; remember the shape made by the rays of the feather and the soft effect given by these. Use the tool to give some indication of the surface caused by their structure.

If you cannot visualise this, find a feather, look at it, really look. Touch each feather in wonder. Then if it helps, try to draw it, thinking of sections through, etc.

The more you know about the construction of the things you carve the better. Such knowledge helps you to see things you would otherwise miss and in turn enables you to cope with the actual carving.

To some degree this knowledge has to be used unconsciously. Just look, sketch, etc. and let the knowledge sink into you mind, to be called upon when needed.

The idea must not be to copy slavishly a natural thing, fish, flesh, fowl or plant. Rather, try to digest what you see, looking at all things as a potential subject for carving.

I know I have said this before, but just as one builds a vocabulary of words as a child, you must build a vocabulary of form. Practically anything seen can add to this if you look at it with this idea in mind.

I find this above is probably the most difficult thing for students of any age or status to grasp. Once they do, things improve rapidly.

Fig. 5. Area 'B' denotes the left-hand wing which is just a little farther away from the viewer. This should be lowered a little and the outer portion worked to a curved plane.

Area
B

62

Fig. 6. An impression of the carving as it would appear in an advanced stage.

Fig. 7. Here the left eye has been given a 'sight' to show contrast with 'unsighted' right eye.

To complete the work insert a 'sight' into the eyes. This is shown in *fig. 7*, and is a small hollow cut in the eyeball with the 'sight' a small point of timber left. The action of light and shade caused by this gives life to the eyes.

When you have taken the work through all these stages, look and if necessary do any further cleaning up and finishing. Wax polish and elbow-grease will be the best finish. Fix a mirror-plate to the back finally so that the work may be hung on the wall.

Fig. 1

EARLY GOTHIC LEAF

Our subject this time is a typical early Gothic leaf. Such foliage was probably based on the leaf of the vine. Later examples show this basis much more clearly.

Some very fine examples of this type of carving can be found in churches all over the British Isles. The subject with a list of churches to visit is covered more extensively under Mediaeval Carved Woodwork in England and Wales in the section on where to view examples in Great Britain on page 127.

As you will see from the design, the early example is based on a square. This is elongated at one corner to form a stalk.

The material used for the example is Japanese Oak, which as I have said previously is the kindest and most amenable of the oak tribe.

Minimum size: 115mm (4½in) long by 90mm (3½in) wide ex 25mm (1in) in thickness.

Extra length if possible will help by giving room for a 'G' cramp and packing piece to hold the work whilst carving is in progress. The extra can be removed with a saw, leaving the appropriate margin on completion.

Draw the design on the face side of your wood and run a depth-line along the sides and ends 9mm (⅜in) from the face side.

Lines A and B may be sawn in with a tenon saw; remember to stop on the depth-line. (*See fig. 2*)

Lower the background as in previous exercises.

Working from the end of the wood towards lines A and B, with a gouge of No. 6 section, ⅝in wide will remove the bulk of the background quickly there. You may have to persuade the process by working diagonally across the grain. The timber will tell you; if it tears try another direction of cut.

Should you have spare wood in the length, another saw cut can be used to terminate the stalk, but do not mark the background. Too deep a cut will show, so stop a little short of the depth-level and the stalk end can be taken to the required depth with a gouge later. Working in this way, removing the

Project

Fig. 1. A simplified Gothic Style leaf.

Fig. 2. Lines 'A' and 'B' may be cut in with a tenon saw, being careful to stop at the depth line marked around the edges.

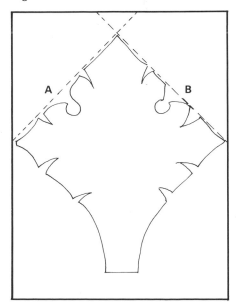

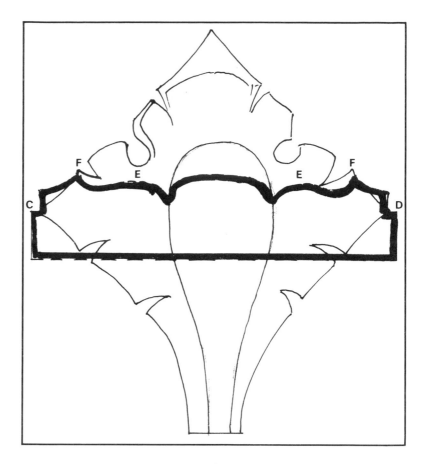

Fig. 3. Section through leaf width from 'C' to 'D' shows full rounded centre and high points of each leaf foil.

background bulk will make the next stage, 'setting-in', easier.

Select the appropriate gouges for this stage, make sure they are sharp, and proceed.

Interpretation

Gothic-style carving is a much more robust affair than the classical Acanthus dealt with previously.

Also, as you may find in possible future exercises following the development of mediaeval carving, the craftsmen of that period had a very strong sense of humour which often shows in their work.

Backgrounds in this period are not highly finished and tool marks do show in moderation. Gouges section 3 or 4 will give the result required for background finish. The leaf centre is raised, so allow this part to remain at full thickness for the present.

Establish its shape by parting-tool or setting-in, then leave that part for now.

The section across the leaf as shown in *fig. 3* is a full rounded centre. Out of the surrounding depression the section rises to each leaf-foil in a curve, then this, after the crest at 'E', sweeps down and up again to leave high points at 'F'.

Fig. 4. This sketch of the finished carving shows clearly how the design is based on a square and how one corner is elongated to form a stalk.

Completion to the end of the foils is a crisper concave plane away from the centre-line of each.

The circular shapes which separate the leaf-foils on sides 'A' and 'B' should be left high. The aim should be, a robust interpretation giving plenty of light and shade.

Explore the form as revealed in the photograph of the example, and shown by the design shading.

Give a slight chamfer effect to leaf edges; this adds to the strength of the interpretation.

Outer edges may now be very slightly undercut below chamfer level. The amount will reveal itself by trial and error, so do not try to achieve too much too soon. Start with only a small amount of undercut, look at the effect and only increase this if you consider it advisable.

Leaf veins are incised; it is better in most instances to set in the vee required; using a parting tool may in this case cause tearing. The centre vein will be the deepest and widest; give it a slight curve to add vigour.

Go over the subject, adding any further finishing touches which you feel are necessary.

Finish off with wax polish. Brush it with a stiff brush to remove excess from crevices, etc. Finally a rub with a duster.

Fig. 5. Another example of early Gothic relief seen at Pengham Church.

LATER DEVELOPMENTS IN MEDIEVAL CARVED WOODWORK

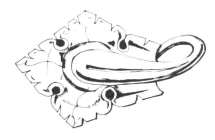

Fig. 1. Variations of vine-leaf shape. Above (top) this early 16th century example can be viewed at the Church of St Thomas of Canterbury at Lapford, North Devon. Above: A stylized version of a vine leaf, based on an example to be seen in Llanrwst Church, Denbighshire.

Fig. 2. Below: A fine example of Medieval-style carved vine in oak.

In this exercise we venture farther along the path of Gothic style carving and look at later developments in that period. The design used in the previous exercise was as I explained loosely based on the leaf of the vine.

In later medieval work foliage developed to show more clearly this basis; also grapes, tendrils and running stems are used. Indeed this type of decoration is called 'Running Vine.' *Fig. 1* shows the progression by stylization from the natural leaf to a 16th century example of running vine. Examples are to be found in the work in the church at Llanrwst, Denbighshire. This type of ornament was used on the mouldings to the heads of church screens.

West Country screens show a great variety of 'running' patterns. The basic outline shape of the leaf is five sided, pentagonal, but variations of this shape-theme do occur.

At Lapford in Devon for example, the basic shape to the leaf is almost a square. Here also the axis of the leaf is horizontal rather than inclined.

The grapes here are smaller, forming not so much bunches as small clusters.

Vine is generally to be found on the Bressummer face. This is a beam which is a structural member used to help support the Rood Lofts surmounting screens. In most examples they run the entire length of the screen. The moulded face lends itself well to this kind of decoration; in some instances two different foliage types appear on the face.

Fig. 3

Project: 'Running Vine' Motif

Fig. 3. Shows a vine-leaf springing from the main stem with grapes emerging from under the leaf on the right. The design is enclosed by the curve of the main stem.

Fig. 4. Section through wood before carving is commenced.

The design to be tackled in this exercise shows a vine-leaf springing from the main stem. This stem also gives rise to the tendril, the means by which the plant climbs and hangs onto its support in nature, in the upper left-hand corner, and grapes emerging from under the leaf to the right-hand. The design is enclosed by the curve of the main stem.

Material
The wood used in the example is Lime, but all the work I did in this style in the years, alas now gone, of great demand for carved decoration to church furnishing was in Oak.

Should you wish to use Oak, Japanese will be the easiest to cut. Beech would be suitable or even Sycamore, not to mention the kinder members of the Mahogany tribe.

Beginnings
It is advisable in some types of work to bring the wood to a simple section throughout its length before even drawing on the design. This is one such occasion and the wood should be planed to the section shown in *fig. 4*.

The size of the example is 125mm (5in) long by 74mm (2⅞in) wide and out of 1in or approx. 25mm thick. A little extra length will help in holding the wood and this can be squared off to size on completion.

When the wood has been sectioned as above, transfer the design to the curved surface. The curve will result in a slightly wider surface than the block size. Such small adjustment to the design as may be needed to cope with this is best dealt with by a slight increase, a widening of the top and bottom margins to the edges.

When the design is to be clearly seen on the curved surface, run a depth-line around the edges and ends of the wood.

This should give a maximum depth at the centre of the section of three-eighths of an inch, about 12mm. Measure this down at the centre and note the measurement of the remainder below. Use the remainder as the depth-line amount when drawing this in from the square surface of the base, not the curve, at the top of the block.

Setting In
This should be done as described in earlier exercises. First select gouges of appropriate section curvature to fit the lines of the design.

The gouge or chisel should be changed to cope with the variation of curve etc. found in these lines.

The first to be set in are those of the perimeter, the outer line only. Do not, at this stage, deal with any of the interior lines in the design. Remove a little on the outside, i.e. the waste side of this perimeter. This will indicate the mass of relief to be carved.

Using a gouge No. 5 or 6 in section and of the width you consider to be best, take this outer background area down to within 2mm (¹⁄₁₆in) of the depth-line.

Complete the process to the line with gouges of shallower section Nos. 3 or 4. The result should now be the queer-shaped island shown in *fig. 5*.

This is a rather dull looking object now, but can be made to appear much more interesting by the setting in and removal of wood to the background level in the shapes within this shape.

One important instance is the almost ovoid shape created by the loop of the leaf-stalk departing from the main stem and passing into the leaf itself. Set in the outline of this shape and remove a little wood from within and up to this line. This gives an appearance similar to a moat surrounding a flat-topped hill. Remove wood from the top of this hill and gradually reduce it to the background level.

There are two smaller loops in the tendrils, set in these and deal with them in a similar way. Also there is a small crescent-shaped part to be set in. Trying to take so small an area as this latter down to background level may present problems. It would be best to press in a central line within the crescent and to push cuts from the outer lines of the shape towards this.

Home-made tools
In other words, 'vee it in' for now. A small 'grounding tool' will help in tight shapes such as this, should you possess one. Many students make their own. These tools are narrow chisels ground to give a slight crank at the cutting end and are used

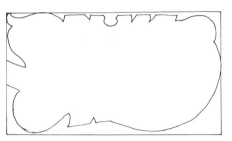

Fig. 5. Perimeter outline to be set in and background lowered.

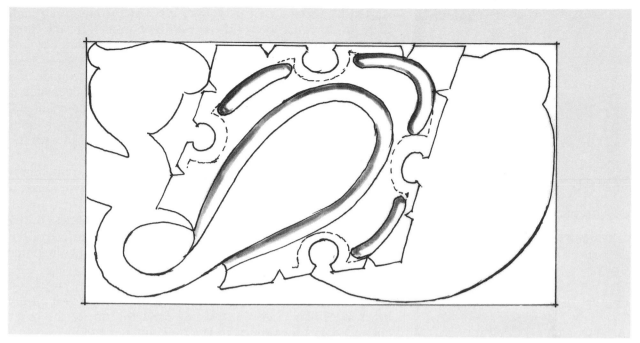

Fig. 6. The first stages in the development of the leaf surface form.

with the bevel underneath in contact with the wood. Pushing this bevel along the surface has a planing action which removes the unwanted material easily.

Such tools are sold in varying end-widths, the ends being forged to spread in a fish-tail shape. These are possibly better for finishing larger backgrounds but I personally rarely use the ones I have.

Many of my part-time students are endeavouring to cope with the costly tools problem and are in some instances making their own. Some have even succeeded in making gouges from old files. Perhaps you could try for yourself, this is merely a suggestion.

The top line of the leaf will now be almost completely delineated; continue this process until the entire leaf shape is set-in. Remember, not too deep where the right-hand edge passes over grapes; do not burst any!

Take a little wood away on the outside of and up to the leaf outline to establish this.

Go over the lines of the tendril. Look at the design and remove a little wood at the places where one curve is shown to pass under another. In the upper portion of the tendril the lower edge is slightly overlaid by the main curve. Try to convey this.

Interpretation of Form

The leaf centre is to be isolated for the time being and should be left at block surface height for now.

This, the beginning of the leaf surface form development, is

Fig. 7. A more stylised variation of vine leaves arranged into a symmetrical design.

Fig. 8. Two variations of the vine leaf carved by the author to be used as roof bosses for the Lady Chapel of Sheffield Cathedral.

started by using a narrow gouge, three sixteenths of an inch wide for the inner loop and one eighth of an inch for the three narrow, smaller shapes. The section to be either number 6 or 7.

Make a channel with the wider one; this surrounds the centre of the leaf. Do not cut it too deep, it can be deepened if necessary later. Carve the smaller shapes as lesser channels. The result should be as shown in *fig. 6*. The broken lines linking these shapes also shown on this are pressed in with the appropriate gouges.

Remove a little wood on the inner side of these, remembering that the inner form to the leaf-foils rises and becomes a rounded shape.

The centre of the leaf should now have the harshness of the raw edges to the channel removed. Work on the surface of the centre part until a soft roundness is achieved; allow the outer edges of the channel to remain rising for now.

The raised leaf-foil centres will require further work on them to soften these and to allow them to sweep down on the inner sides. They will in so doing meet the rise of the outer channel edges mentioned in the previous paragraph.

Work over the entire surface of the leaf until the forms flow together. The design shows this.

Grapes

The outer lines of the bunch of grapes, those to the right and bottom, may now be set in. The surface of the main stem curving around these should be lowered in height. This will allow the grapes to stand in higher relief.

The individual outlines of the grapes are set in. Now, by working away from the highest parts, carve the surfaces into the set-in lines. In this way the necessary rounded shape will be given to the surface of the fruit.

The smaller stalk from which the bunch of grapes hangs can be shaped. Give this an appearance to show a defined joint with the main stem.

From the foregoing written instructions, together with study of the design and other diagrams and with the photograph of the finished work in front of you, continue until the work is completed.

As a finishing touch the outer edges of leaf, stem and tendril may be slightly undercut. The emphasis being on the word slightly; we are dealing with Gothic not Grinling.

Before leaving the work of the Gothic period, it is worth mentioning that work from the late medieval period can be seen on the continent of Europe. There are excellent examples of woodcarving to be found in the churches and museums of the Netherlands and Germany.

EARLY 17TH CENTURY FURNITURE DECORATION

This chapter and exercise are in response to the many requests I get for information on the carved decoration used on furniture dating from 16th and 17th centuries.

The latter half of the 15th century and early 16th saw the development of the last phase of the Gothic period in architecture. This is called the 'Perpendicular' style culminating in such masterpieces as Kings College Chapel, Cambridge (1446-1515), St George's Chapel, Windsor and other examples.

Here we see the development of the Gothic style in England almost free from outside influences. Until this final flowering the various Gothic phases had arrived here around 100 years after their earliest manifestations on the continental mainland of Europe.

Once they arrived here they became Anglicised, but the 'Perpendicular' style would appear to be indigenous to this country. Should you ever be able to visit the above mentioned churches they are most rewarding.

Just stand in Kings College for example and looking up behold the wonder and glory of the fan-vaulting overhead, remembering as you do so that such structures were not the work of architects in the modern usage of the word.

The architect of such structures allied his undoubted artistic gifts to many years of practical experience as a mason. A master mason with a sound knowledge of geometry, with the ability to put his ideas into designs, and to prepare the plans, elevations and details necessary to bring those ideas to fruition. He had knowledge of costing and was in overall charge of the project. With him would be the master carpenter. The names of some of these remarkable men are known and the sketch-book of one master mason does in fact survive.

Renaissance
The process of Anglicisation, if there could be such a word, continued into the periods following Gothic, Tudor and Elizabethan. Oak was still the material used and this also affords a link with the previous periods.

Some authorities give the dates of these styles as Tudor 1519-1603, the latter part of this (1558-1603) being classified as Elizabethan.

Eventually this gave rise to the style called Jacobean (1603-1649). These are all very much a hybrid of late Gothic and very early Renaissance influences.

The full effect of the Renaissance was not apparent in this country until 18th Century and was then largely the result of ideas brought home by the sons of the well-to-do returning from the European Grand Tour.

The styles have a period of transition between one and the next succession, and dates cannot really be rigidly accepted because of the time overlap. This in itself varying in different parts of Britain.

Examples of Gothic-Renaissance transitional decoration can be seen in some church woodwork.

One instance which comes to mind is to be seen in Lapford Church, North Devon. Here bench-ends have Gothic tracery but this encloses shield-like shapes decorated with Italianate scrolls surmounted by the heads of fantastic beasts.

Other evidences of early Renaissance in the West Country are at Broomfield and in Milverton in Somerset. Swimbridge and Pilton in Devon have also good examples from this period.

The Victoria and Albert Museum, London, Dept of Woodwork has excellent examples of 16th Century decoration. I recall two bench-ends the provenance of which is 'from a Devonshire Church'. One example has had some restoration to a bottom panel at a later date.

These examples make use of scroll-like leaves and heads, one of these being quite like that of a parrot. The other depicts dolphinesque creatures emerging from the scroll leaves at the panel-top.

Decorative elements of 16th century

Much use of strap-work, carved to suggest that this inter-weaves at various points along the rails of furniture, dates from that time. The space available often dictates the design used.

Flatness is the overall impression, all decoration being cut in low-relief. Some examples have a simplified leaf motif, very often consisting of vee-lines only. These are the result of either setting in or the use of a parting-tool with its vee section.

The result does sometimes appear to bear a very slight resemblance to the medieval 'running foliage' type of decoration dealt with earlier but is crude by comparison.

Some circular and semi-circular motifs are incorporated. These are elaborated in various ways by the use of gouges, sometimes giving only flattened hollows radiating from the centre of each unit. At other times a little more detail is used, having for the design-source flower shapes. These are made to

Fig. 1. Upper part of Court Cupboard, early 17th century (Jacobean). Reproduced by kind permission of the Victoria and Albert Museum.

fit into the circles, half-circles or rectangular shapes enclosed by the strap-work.

Heavy turned balusters are characteristic of the period. These are often decorated with gadroons and very simplified leaves. They occur on court-cupboards and tables at the latter end of the 16th century and early 17th century.

Again an excellent example is to be found in the Victoria and Albert Museum. A court-cupboard made in the manner typical of its date of 1610 and with a set-back to the upper part. The top of this upper portion is the full depth of the piece thereby giving a large overhang. This is supported by two turned and decorated balusters, large in girth to their centre parts as shown in illustration.

On the crown of this portion are carved gadroons giving a good effect of light and shade. Below this is turned moulding and below this there are vertical leaves carved in a simple but very effective manner. The tops and bottoms of the balusters are of much smaller diameter with shell-like motifs carved on the base collets.

To return to the actual top of the court-cupboard, this has a plain moulded capping with a rail to front and end returns below it.

The decoration to the face of the rail is strap-work similar to that shown in the illustration. The face of the set-back upper region has a decorated centre flanked on either side by a carved pilaster. Cupboards, one at each side of this centre, have doors with what appears to be incised linear decoration.

The pilasters have ionic capitals and shaped shafts which almost echo the lines of the balusters. Their front faces are elaborately carved using some of the motifs of the strap-work but possibly deeper cut.

The centre panel within these has an arch with spandrels and resting on flat faced pilasters. These and the arch have

Fig. 2. Baluster with gadroon and simplified leaves characteristic of the period.

75

strap-work decoration of interlacing circles. Below the set-back, when the piece of furniture returns to full depth, there are two large cupboards. These have framed and panelled doors without carved decoration.

Over these the work has a fairly large ovolo moulding to front and ends. This is decorated with semi-circular motifs of the type mentioned earlier.

Another device used in this period, but not on this example, was the linen-fold panel. An early example, showing possibly the beginnings of linen-fold in this country, is to be found in a church in Buckinghamshire.

I have never had the opportunity to visit North Crawley but bench-ends in the church look interesting from the reference available.

Panels in these ends are moulded to a section very like that necessary for linen-fold. However for some reason these moulded surfaces have never been carved and grounded to complete the linen-fold appearance.

Fig. 3. Decoration to a rail, based on a court cupboard dated 1610.

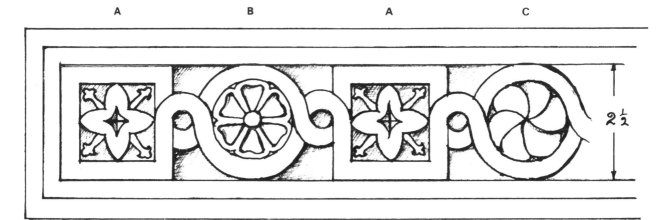

Project: Strapwork Decoration

The subject for the present exercise is an example of the strap-work used as decoration at the beginning of the 17th century.

This is based on the carving found on the court-cupboard mentioned above.

I would suggest that the actual carving be 65mm (2½in) wide on a rail of 100m (4in) approx depth. The length can be to fit the material you have as a trial or a rail of specific size.

The design shows square units which are repeated along with the smaller circular linking device. The larger circles are of constant size but their infilling should be varied using perhaps alternate designs or an even greater amount of variation if you wish. Two examples are shown but no doubt with practice other ideas may occur to you for use along with these.

With pencil and paper try a few doodles, using a square grid of lines as a basis. Fitting the square and circular shapes into this frame-work may help you to make a start. If you do come

EARLY 17TH CENTURY FURNITURE DECORATION

up with an idea scale it up to the size required and keep it by you. This can be used for exercise or after you have tried the present one.

For the present exercise, find some material, preferably Japanese oak, and draw the design on one side of this.

Procedure

The outer lines, i.e., those of the rectangle to enclose the ornament, can be cut with a parting-tool leaving the actual corners to be set in and Vee-d with flat chisels.

Set in the outer lines only of the circular elements for the present. The background is to be lowered not more than 6mm (¼in). Do this by first removing the background side of these lines to clarify which is to be lowered and which is to stay.

Lower each small background area carefully and if you have the cranked grounding tools mentioned earlier, use these to get into and clear corners and other shapes. Do not forget the interior to the smaller circles. These main background shapes will have a punched finish, but more of that later.

Position 'A' on the design shows the content of the squares. Set these lines in carefully and remove the background to 3mm, ⅛in depth. Be careful with the four lance-like shaped diagonals; these could be fragile.

They will be lowered very slightly from the main face. The main quatrefoil shape being left at face level. The centres being a pocket as in chip-carving, but with the sides of these diamond-shapes very slightly curved.

To do this, use a small flat chisel, tilt so that the centre will be cut deeper and press-in. Next shave off the four inclined planes to the slight curve shown. The depth to be a comfortable out-come of this process. *Do not overdo it. No 'quarrying'.*

The content of the circular motifs 'B' can now be tackled. The inner line of the strap should be set in very lightly for now with the smaller curves to each petal top emphasized just a little.

The very small triangle shapes between each petal at the rim are sloped. Think of the flower lying within a saucer-like shape. This will obviate trying to give such a small shape a flat level background.

Press in with the appropriate gouge the small circular centre to each floret. The petals should be hollowed slightly with edges left to the shapes shown in the drawing. Press a small amount off each radiating line to give a slightly inclined surface falling to stop at the small centre boss.

Continue these processes until unit 'C' is reached. In this the petals appear to overlap. Deal with the outer edges as in 'B', then press in the curves of the overlapping edges.

Carve each petal surface lightly to give the impression that each near edge passes under the leading edge of the petal next to it.

77

Fig. 1. Red Indian Chief. A Profiled relief carving in Lime captures the distinctive features of a Redskin.

PROFILE RELIEF CARVING

This profile relief was done in response to a request for a for a wall plaque of a Red Indian for a child's bedroom.

The wall plaques I have carved over the years have been 'profiled reliefs'. In these the subject is profiled by sawing and carving to the outline, then mounted on a back board to enable the work to be safely secured whilst carving.

The design may be suggested by a bird, animal, flower or figure but should be thought of as a design without too great an attempt at unnecessary detail being made.

For this present exercise the design will show the simplification. This applies especially to the feathering of the head-dress.

The profile of the face should be strong, the nose aquiline, eagle-like. Think of the 'Thunder Bird' depicted on the totem poles of some of the Redskin tribes.

The eye is very important too, but more of that later. Keep the outline of the whole design strong and robust.

Material
The example is in Lime but many timbers are carvable. Use nothing with an awkward grain of course. Japanese Oak, Mahogany (not Sapele), Beech, etc. will all fill this bill.

Profiling
This may be done with a coping saw or others of similar type. Failing this, use a technique similar to the one suggested in the exercise 'in the round'. With a tenon saw place cuts at strategic points around the outline. Then cut in towards these and gradually find the outline. Use a vice to hold the work and remove the excess wood around the perimeter of the design.

Backing
In order to hold the profiled work whilst carving, it must be mounted on a backing piece. Blockboard will be useful for this, not too large in size but enough to take the relief and 'G' cramp.

Project:
A Wall Plaque

79

However the problem is just how to fix the work in such a way that it can be removed from the backing piece when completed. The answer is simple. Glue a piece of paper flat onto one side of the blockboard. Newspaper will do, but I prefer something a little thicker. Cartridge paper is better: use old discarded sketches and drawings or outworn covering sheets used on the drawing board as underlays to the tracing and detail paper used for most of the drawings, designs, etc.

When this 'mounting paper' is dry and the wood to be carved fully profiled, put some glue on to the flat back surface of this. Now mount this on the papered board and apply enough pressure to seal it. Leave until the glue is set and in the waiting period sharpen tools in readiness for the next stage.

If you have not made a tracing of the design, make one now. Some of the lines on the subject will be removed in carving. A tracing will enable you to locate the position of any such lines when it is necessary to redraw these.

Carving, beginning Fig. 2, Point A

This shows the starting place to carve a rounded form to the leading edge of the head-dress. Using a fairly flat sectioned gouge gives this rounded form to the edge from point 'A' to 'A1'.

B to B1 on this illustration indicates the top of the headband. Carve in this line using the parting tool, i.e., the vee-sectioned tool described previously. When this has been done,

Fig. 2. With the profile already cut out, this illustration shows the starting place to carve a rounded form to the leading edge of the head dress. The top of the headband is indicated by the heavier line B to B1.

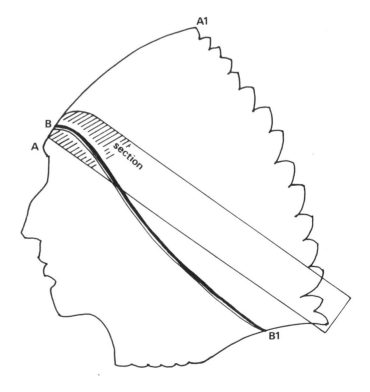

80

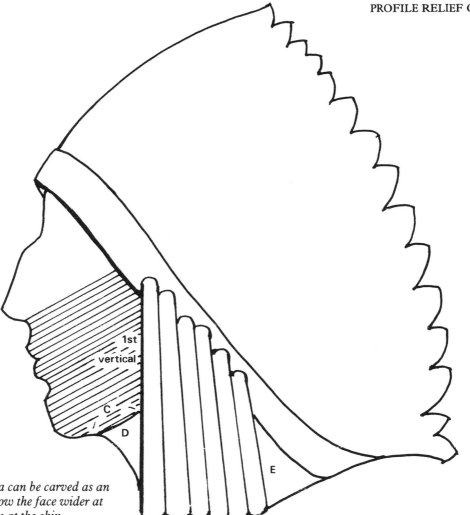

Fig. 3. Shaded area can be carved as an inclined plane to show the face wider at the cheek bones than at the chin.

place the tracing of the subject in correct position and reinstate any of the setting out lines which may have been removed. A small portion of line B to B1 will have been replaced freehand before using the parting tool.

In a similar manner carve the lines of the lower edge of the headband stopping at the first vertical of the decorative falls. This is shown as a heavier line in *fig. 3.*

Put in this first vertical, again with the parting tool, and continue with the remaining vertical lines.

Find a small gouge and set in the tops of the falls and with one slightly less in curve, deal with their terminations.

If the first vertical is deepened, the lower part being of greater depth, the area shaded on *fig. 3.* can be carved as an inclined plane dropping approximately 4mm (⅛in) to the jaw-line. The fall at this part may be increased later but for now leave plenty of material for the chin.

This plane is to convey the fact that the face is wider at the cheek bones that at the chin.

81

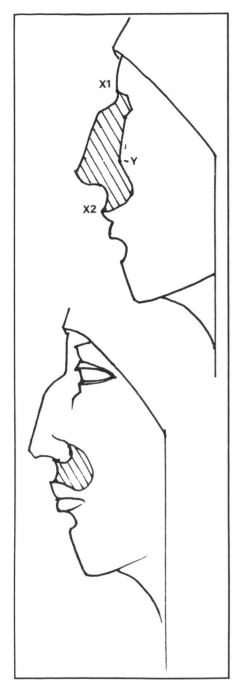

Fig. 4. Above (top): Maintain the fine profile of the aquiline nose by dealing with the area X1–X2 first. The whole of the portion shaded is lowered by 3mm. Fig. 5. Above: Shaded area indicates where small amount of wood should be removed to leave a slightly concave plane.

The smaller triangular area under the chin, show as 'D' on *Fig. 3*, is another inclined plane. The tilt is from under the jaw down to the lower point of the triangle. If a slightly hollow depression is given to this plane where it reaches the jawline, this will give the small amount of emphasis required here.

At the right-hand of the 'falls' is another area, again triangular in shape at point 'E'. This can be lowered by 5mm (³⁄₁₆in) approximately. This is part of the neck showing behind the falls and up to the lower edge of the headband. Remember then that it must show some relationship to the other plane at 'D'.

The features of the face

As we have noted these should give an impression of strength. *Fig. 4* position X1-X2 shows the part to be dealt with first.

Press in, using the appropriate gouge section along this line which passes in front of the eye, down along the front of the cheek bone, then turns out to join the profile at the top of the upper lip. The depth should be greater from X1 to Y and remember the area behind this line will be highest, so incline the cut slightly from the higher to the lower level in front. The remainder of the line, passing at first slightly back then making a change of direction before ending, should be pressed in very lightly.

Lower the whole of the portion shaded by 3mm (⅛in).

Draw on this new surface the shape of the wing of the nose, that is, the lower part cloaking the nostril and leaving this at *Fig. 4* height.

Press the outline in as shown in *Fig. 5* and remove a small amount of wood as the shading here shows, making a slightly concave plane. Do not press in the lines indicating this small area, rather use these as, at the top of the lip, an edge to the concave plane and a starting place from which to carve this.

The tonal illustration (*figs.* 6, 7) will I trust convey the various surfaces, etc. arrived at now in the facial area. The two lines of the upper and line one of the lower or bottom eyelid may now be pressed in and the front line of these and the eye itself established.

Try to remember that the eye does close and allow enough thickness to the upper eyelid to give this impression.

Two vee cuts across are insufficient to convey this and yet this is the method adopted by many. Give some depth to the profile of the eye and the eyelids so that even seen in profile they do have some fullness of form.

Details of the features

The mouth; press in the actual line of the opening, then work the curved planes of the upper and lower lips into this line. Give the curves to these, look at the illustrations, *fig. 6* and 7. The latter is an advancement on *fig. 6*, the lips have been reduced a little in size by working on the various planes cut to deal with the surrounding form.

The details of the eye are shown and a 'sight' added. This latter is cut in such a way as to use the action of light to give life to the eye.

At art college, 'Drawing from the antique' was an important part of the curriculum for my generation. Full size plaster casts of Greeks and Graeco-Roman sculpture had to be drawn and drawn until they haunted our dreams.

However to return to our point, such works are invariably 'blind', that is, no light and shade enlivens their eyes.

The tonal rendering drawn will I trust help to clarify the above. Smaller planes are used as the work progresses and will show, I hope, on the photograph of the completed work.

The head-dress
The band of serrated lines above the head-band is used to show smaller feathers and these should now be set in with gouges of appropriate size and section.

This done, remove a very slight amount of wood from around the tops of these to establish their position.

The longer feathers must now be dealt with, a parting tool may help. Try it, if unsuccessful set in the lower edge of each feather with the necessary tools. Remember that they overlie each other from top to bottom so that apart from the top one, each upper edge is cloaked by the feather above.

When the shapes are made clear, tool the surfaces of each feather with a number 3 or 4 section gouge. The facets left will enliven the surfaces.

The 'falls', decorative leather strips or twisted cord-like shapes make a series of verticals. You will have already positioned these. Give each of them a rounded effect and using a small parting tool add to the decoration as is shown in the design and example.

Check your carving against the design, if your work is completed to that but you feel any additions of your own are necessary, put them in.

Go round all the edges and replace any saw cuts remaining with gouge texture. When you are satisfied, place a flat chisel, bevel down on to the block-board. The best position would probably be at the base of the design.

Tap gently until the thin edge of the chisel goes under between carving and back-board. Press the tool handle end down and the paper will split allowing the carving to come free.

Sand off the back to remove any paper remaining. Clean the edges and finish the carving with wax or other polish.

All that remains now is to put a glass or mirror plate or other means of hanging in the back.

I trust that your children will appreciate your efforts.

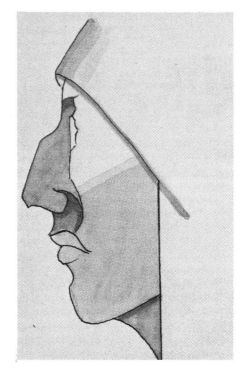

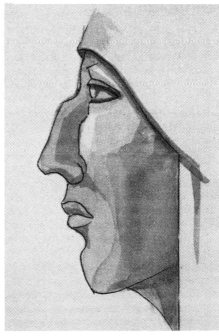

Fig. 6. Above (top): The tonal areas indicate various surfaces to be arrived at as the carving reaches an advanced stage.
Fig. 7. Above: is a further advancement on fig. 6.

LETTERING: CLASSICAL ROMAN

This is a very important subject yet I deal with it only rarely when teaching in Adult Education Centres or privately. Here I will attempt to give some introduction to the subject and then move on to the practical matter of letter shapes etc. and the cutting thereof.

There are many styles and types of lettering, some good, some bad and some shocking. Letters which are ornate or over-elaborated are difficult to read and legibility should be the prime requirement of any lettering.

Over the years I must have carved thousands of letters. The vast majority of these have been of the 'Incised' type and this exercise will deal with that type of lettering.

When an architect or designer has furnished a full-size drawing of requirements, this has always been adhered to. However, when the setting-out has been left to me, Classical Roman has been the lettering used. There are many variations to be found even within the field of Roman lettering itself. At the time when I was a student one particular inscription was used as the basis for all instruction in the subject.

That inscription is to be found on a panel at the base of the Trajan Column in Rome. The drawing and the analysis of proportions, shape and construction of the letters in this inscription occupied at least two hours per week of our time throughout the first year syllabus.

This will, I trust, give you some small idea of the amount of background knowledge then considered necessary. A student at that time was not allowed to attempt to cut any lettering in either wood or stone until that first year was fully completed.

The Trajan Column inscription
This is generally accepted to be the finest surviving example of the letter-cutter's art known to the western world.

There is a very good example in Britain but it has had to be much restored. This example was discovered by Professor Donald Atkinson in 1924 in 169 fragments at the Roman Site of Viroconium (Wroxeter) in Shropshire. It is now in Shrewsbury Museum. It was, as far as is known, originally over the gateway to the Forum at Viroconium.

In spite of the condition in which it was found the panel is a thing of great beauty and the restorer has done an excellent job considering the magnitude of the task then before him.

To return to the Trajan column example. This was carved in marble around the year 114 A.D. It is 18ft, getting on for 6 metres, above ground in a horizontal position at the base of the column. The size of the panel is just over 9ft, roughly 3 metres long and 3ft 9in, just over 1 metre high. The name of the letter-cutter is, of course, unknown but his work has been a source of admiration and inspiration over the centuries.

The following letters do not occur in the inscription, H; J (as we know it), K; U (as we know it), W, Y and Z. But when the existing letters have been studied it is possible to arrive at satisfactory shapes and proportions for these.

Unusual characteristics

There are many small things in the inscription which, though possibly a little strange to the purely logical mind, nevertheless do add to the beauty of the work.

One of these occurs in the letter 'A', the two inclined legs of which vary very slightly in the angle made by them and the horizontal general base-line to the lettering. Also the apex of this letter projects very slightly above the top of the horizontal line of the lettering. Such slight variations need not be slavishly followed; indeed, I do not use them myself in this letter, but they are present in the original.

Another such example, and one which I do follow always, occurs in the letter 'O'. The central upright axis of this leans slightly against the line of march of the letters. A very slight incline to the left. The angle made by this axis and the baseline is 82° instead of 90° vertical.

In the letter 'S' the vertical axis leans with the line of march. A very slight incline to the right.

The round letters such as 'C' and 'D' appear to have a slight bagging or heaviness to the bottom of their curves.

These and other little deviations from the absolutely logical occur in many letters of this inscription. They give character and add to the grace and beauty of this legacy left to us by a letter-cutter of Imperial Rome.

Serifs

These are terminals, ends, or feet used to stabilize or complete the letters. See sketch.

They do not occur on the tops of the inclined strokes of 'N's and 'M's in the Trajan example.

There is a precedent for such usage in an inscription found in North Street, Chichester. This example is very good, but I prefer not to use serifs on these letters in these positions.

Reproduced by kind permission of the Victoria and Albert Museum, London.

Fig. 1. Letters redrawn from the Roman inscription found at Wroxeter, Shropshire. The original, much restored, is now in Shrewsbury Museum.

Fig. 2. Inscription on the Trajan Column in Rome. This is generally accepted to be the finest surviving example of the letter-cutter's art known to the Western World.

Proportions

One important thing to remember about Roman lettering is that it is based, in the first instance, on the action of a reed or quill pen. The natural outcome of the use of either of these gives a thin up-stroke and a thick down-stroke to letters. If this is kept in mind it will help.

The thickness of the wide-stroke is one tenth of the height of the letters. Thin strokes are half the width of these.

These proportions do vary a little in some letters, but the above is a reasonable working rule. In the six rows of lettering which make up the Trajan inscription, the heights of the letters are staggered slightly to compensate for the angle of viewing.

As already stated, the apex of the letter 'A' does project slightly above the general height-line of the letters. The cross-stroke, which after all stabilizes that letter, should not, I feel, be placed too high.

Again, such details are for personal selection. In the letter 'B' the lower curve is slightly bolder than that of the upper part.

'C' can be drawn with compasses but remember the inclined axis and its effect on thicks and thins. See notes for letter 'O'.

Regarding the serifs which terminate the letter 'C', try not to get these too big. The one at the top is slightly larger than the lower one; indeed, the lower end of the curve is sometimes left without a serif in other inscriptions.

'D' again, use compasses; the slight 'bagging' mentioned above is not an absolute necessity in the lettering you are ever likely to do.

In 'E', the central cross-stroke I place above and resting on the centre-line of letter height. 'F' is similar. The length of these mid-strokes I shorten, giving a slight step back in both letters. The overall width of these two letters can be just a little under half the height.

'M' again has the apices very slightly above general height as found in the 'A'. As already stated, I do not give serifs to the tops of these.

'N' also has this height characteristic at its left-hand and this again has no serif to the point.

Regarding the widths of these letters, try not to allow them to sprawl, on the other hand do not get them too narrow.

Remember the slight lean out of absolute vertical given to the axis of letter 'O'. The thinnest parts of this letter occur at the top and bottom of this axis. The thickest occur at the position where an axis at 90° to the centre of the main axis touches the circle at each side.

'P' has the upper rounded portion occupying slightly more than half the total height.

'Q' is the 'O' plus the addition of the tail-stroke. 'R' has the top curve coming down slightly below the centre-line of the height. The effect should be a slightly larger curved portion than in the 'P'. The forward stroke has actually a slight curve and no serif but does project very slightly, below the general base-line.

However, a straight stroke at the correct angle and with a serif can be used here; it does help stability. 'S', as has been mentioned, does have this slight forward incline to the vertical centre-line. 'T' is a little less in overall width than in height.

'W', as we have noted, does not occur in the Trajan inscription. Some alphabets show the two middle strokes overlapping. I prefer them to meet at the top in an apex.

'U' is sometimes shown as a thick down-stroke continuing round at the base to become a thin up-stroke. I prefer the second stroke to be thick and to have serifs to top and bottom.

Other letters can be drawn with these basic principles in mind.

I once reviewed a book which advocated the use of a file of triangular section to finish the vee-section of a letter. Will you please *not do this*. Incised lettering is, as its name suggests, the result of a cutting process and the end result must be from this action only. If the process is done correctly there will be no reason whatsoever for any further action.

Spacing

Remember that in any lettering spacing is almost as important as the letters themselves. Letters, and the words they make, must flow in a pleasing and comfortable way.

Spacing is not something which can be measured with a rule, be it metric or imperial. Neither can it be done with a pair of dividers. It must be evident to all of you, that when an open letter, say a 'C', is followed by a vertical such as in 'E',

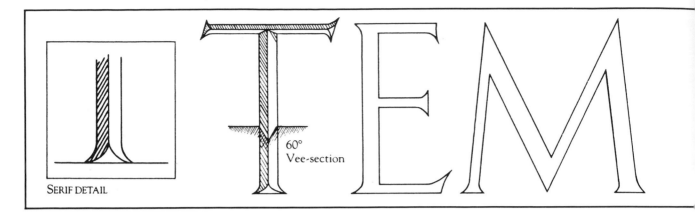

SERIF DETAIL

60°
Vee-section

some of the weight of space within the 'C' must be taken into account.

There are no steadfast rules about this aspect of our subject; good spacing will come with practice. The eye must be trained to assess what looks good and what does not.

The spaces between words require the same visual approach. A reasonable suggestion could be to allow the space which would be occupied by one letter between each word.

However this may be, such space should be sufficient to separate each word from its neighbour but not large enough to interrupt the flow of these words.

Project: Incised Lettering

Cutting, Technique and Practice

For an introduction to the practical aspect of our subject I have set out the word TEMPUS as in 'Tempus Fugit'. The letters involved should afford a variety of experience in the actual cutting of letters.

One point had better be made before we start. As has already been stated here, there are many variations within the field of Roman Lettering and I shall no doubt have readers' comments on this aspect.

This book puts my own experience before you, gained as explained earlier. Should you prefer to follow one or other of the many alphabets based on Roman Lettering to be found in books on the subject, that is for you to choose.

The actual technique of cutting cannot vary greatly in incised letters. You may find your own personal approach to some letter details. Explore these for yourselves, experiment, try out, investigate. *Always* draw in the centre-line to letter thickness.

Materials

The tools to be used should be sharp and No. 1 section flat chisels will be required in various widths.

Gouges will cover a range of section through No. 4 to No. 6 and these too will be required in various widths.

Fig. 3. Roman lettering incised 60° vee-section. Put in centre-lines to all letter strokes before carving.

Oak, Beech and Mahogany are suitable in this instance.

Transfer the lettering to the wood by carbon-film or carbon-paper. Trace the letters on to the tracing paper first. This allows ease in locating the setting-out position on the timber. Fasten this tracing at the top, lift up and slip the carbon film underneath.

Go over the letter outlines and centre-lines, lift up the setting out to check that all lines have been dealt with. If they have, remove the tracing and carbon paper.

'T' is the first letter. Apply a flat chisel of required width vertically to the centre-line of the upright stroke.

Tap in with a mallet.

It is not advisable to use hand pressure alone for this. Lettering is clearly defined; the use of the mallet will help to achieve this decisive quality.

Do not allow the setting in any centre line to intrude into the serif area. If this does occur, a chisel-line will show in the completed letter where no such line should be seen. See sketch.

The angle of the 'Vee-section' of incised letters is 60°. This may require variation on some occasions, i.e. when letters are to be gilded, but 60° is a good working angle.

Make cuts to achieve this section by cutting inclined planes to each side of the centre-cut.

It should not be assumed that the vee section to, say, a vertical stroke is to be the result of two clouts only with a mallet and chisel.

Take your time and remove a little at a time from each side of the vee until a clear clean-sided vee-section is achieved.

The serifs which terminate the ends of the cross-piece of the letter 'T', and that to the bottom of the upright central shaft, are most easily dealt with by using a flat chisel.

Use one about a quarter of an inch, or the metric equivalent, wide. If you should have a small fish-tail flat, this will be better than a tool with parallel sides.

In actual fact, the lines of the bottom of the vee to the outer

Fig. 4. Pierre de Fouchard, Founder of Dental Surgery. Relief in Lime, with raised letters gilded. Plaque mounted on the front of a portable lectern in oak. Work carved by the author for "The Society for the Study of Orthodontics".

corners of the serif are slightly curved, but this refinement may be ignored for ease of execution. Also a flat chisel may be easier to come by and to use for many people.

Press in (hand pressure) with the tool along the centre-lines of the serif, tilting the tool so that the cut is deepest towards the central vertical.

Shave off the triangular shaped inclined plane between these two outer cuts to the depth of the vertical vee-section. Then work the sides of the vertical into those of the serif.

Try for a flowing curve; do not go in for the 'hob-nailed boot' effect seen in some lettering.

Carve the cross-stroke to the 'T' in a similar way, remembering that it is a thin-stroke and also the serifs which terminate this are smaller. The letter 'E' is to be carved using the same technique.

The 'M' will respond to similar measures, but remember that the first stroke is up and therefore a thin-stroke.

The two apices will need care; a small central inclined cut towards the main vertical set-in cut will help. Tilt the small flat chisel to join this main cut at maximum depth.

This should show that central setting-in cuts should not intrude too far into apices in addition to non-intrusion into serifs. For example, the points of the letter 'N'.

The letter 'P' should have the centre lines set in first, using the appropriate gouge size and section to fit the upper rounded portion. Possibly section five or six. In instances like this sections three and four, narrow in width, are very useful.

The letter 'U' in the drawing is as suggested earlier in this text. Tackle this letter as you have the others. Try to obtain the continuity of curve at the bottom and get a clean effect where the right-hand of this curve meets the upright.

The last letter in our present exercise is 'S'. This can be an awkward letter to cut but at the size being dealt with at present should not be beyond your abilities.

It is when very small letters are required that real trouble is experienced.

Make sure that a centre-line is drawn to the curves of the letter. Then select the gouges to fit these, working with the technique suggested for other letters, try to cut this one.

When you have completed the lettering use a fine-grit sandpaper wrapped around a flat-sided cork rubber and dress off the surface. This is to clean the surface and to remove setting-out lines only. Do not apply too much pressure.

Give the whole surface a rub with a bristle nailbrush to clear sanding dust, etc. Apply the polish you generally use. Remember if, for example, shellac is used, the vee-section must not be blurred by too thick a layer of polish. This does occur quite often and too little polish is better by far than too much.

Finish off with a duster.

LETTERING: SANS SERIF

As stated in the last exercise there are many styles of lettering, ranging from the very elaborate to very plain. Among the most elaborate would be the various forms of Gothic script, sometimes designated 'Olde Englishe'. But even this lettering can, if a few of the curlicues are subdued or omitted, be cut as 'incised' letters.

However in this, our present instance, 'block' lettering will have our consideration.

Some examples of this style tend to be heavy in appearance but there is one alphabet which springs to mind as excellent.

This is 'Gill Sans Serif', designed by Eric Gill, a sculptor famous earlier this century. These letters are light in thickness of stroke and very easy to read.

Should you wish to consider this style for yourself, have a look in your local public library. The reference number in library catalogues for lettering in general is 745-6; find books under this number on the shelves.

Remember also to have a look on the shelves of the 'oversize book' section. It is surprising how many books on all subjects are to be found in this category.

The example to be used in the present instance will be based on the Trajan inscription letter-shapes considered in the last chapter.

The one big difference is that in 'block' lettering the widths of the strokes are constant; there are no thicks and thins.

As to the type of letter, 'raised' will be used. In this, as the name suggests, the background is removed to a lower level allowing the letters to stand in relief.

Material

Use a timber which is fairly close-grained and hard enough to keep the edges of the upstand of each letter clean and clear.

Beech is good or one of the Mahoganies, Brazilian for example would do quite well.

Japanese Oak is another suitable timber, pleasant to cut and a good colour.

Project:
Raised Lettering

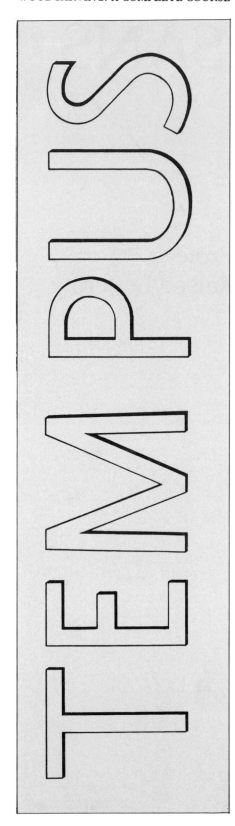

English Oak can be quite hard and wayward having at times a will of its own. It always looks and weathers well when completed.

Sycamore is hard and at times down-right cussed but again looks well once completed.

Size around 285mm 11¼ inches long by 95mm 3¾ inches wide Ex 25mm 1 inch, Plane the wood up, faces and edges, before you set on the letters.

Procedure — setting on

First do a tracing of the letters. The word Tempus is again used as it gives a good variation of letter-shapes and will allow comparison of the two techniques: 'incised' last exercise and 'raised' in this.

Position the tracing of the letters on your material, allowing a slightly larger margin at the bottom than at the top.

Fasten with drawing-pins and put a sheet of carbon paper or film underneath. Transfer the letters to the surface of the wood.

Go over all the lines with a fairly hard pencil, say a '2H'. Lift up the setting out and carbon to check that the lines are all clearly transferred before releasing the setting-out.

Put a line at the required background depth around sides and ends of the wood, then fasten it securely to the bench top with a G-cramp, Bench Holdfast or similar. Use a packing-piece to save marking the wood surface.

Select the tools required, flat chisels of various widths and gouges of the appropriate size and section. Make sure that they are sharp and give them a good final stropping.

Cutting

Set in the edges of each letter, remembering to incline the cuts a little away from the upstand to give the small amount of buttress effect required in these first stages. This procedure was dealt with in the early 'Relief' exercises of this series.

Remove a little of the wood to establish the positions of the letters. Use about a No. 4 section gouge cutting towards and up to the set in outlines.

It does help, when dealing with raised letters on a small size background, to clear the top and bottom margins throughout the length of the wood. Think of them as rebates and a plane could be used in this instance to clear them if you wish. Another way would be to cut in the lines to the top and bottom of the lettering using a parting tool with its vee-section, establishing these lines through the whole length of the wood. The margins can then be lowered to depth with gouges.

Once this is done, start the task of removing the remaining background areas to the depth-line.

Use a No. 6 section gouge about ⅜ inch wide and, starting at the left-hand edge, cut a channel towards and stopping at

Fig. 5. (Opposite) Block lettering 'raised' by lowering surrounding background level a minimum of 4mm to leave letters in relief.

the setting in of the first letter. Cut further channels alongside each other. This will result in the 'ploughed field' effect mentioned in the earlier exercises on 'Relief' carving.

Deal with all the background areas in this way. If this procedure of setting in the outlines prior to the removal of each layer of background area is followed, the progression towards the depth-line around sides and edges will advance, but will do so under your control.

Do not expect to achieve full background depth at one go, be content to progress slowly and steadily.

Be especially careful when dealing with the parts of the background which are within closed or partially closed letters.

When the bulk of wood has been removed with the section No. 6 gouge, change to shallower section, either No. 3 or No. 4, in the appropriate widths required. Finally, finishing the surface to depth-line with the No. 3 gouge will give a lightly textured surface.

Go carefully around the edges of each letter to make these as clean and clear as possible. If you can work with a flat chisel about ⅜ inch wide, positioned on its side and cut along the long edges to the straight letter-strokes, this will help to give them the final clean-up.

Use the tool with the bevel side to the wood to obviate any tendency to run into the actual letter-shape. Incidentally, this is one of the reasons why I suggest one bevel only to flat chisels when sharpening.

Place the wood in a good side-light; this will tend to emphasize any flaws in cutting. View with the light from alternate sides.

Should you wish to try setting out further letters, keep in mind that the drawing of the letters first is of prime importance. Unless the setting-out is satisfactory, carving, no matter how skilful, will tend to be wasted.

With this in mind look at the various alphabets to be found in books on lettering and at those examples from any other source you may find.

It has been suggested that the various transfer letters now on the market may help. (Take a look at Letraset.) Investigate these for yourself and if they appeal, try them.

I do not use these products, so just what styles and sizes are available it will be up to you to discover.

Fig. 1. The official logo of The Guild of Master Craftsmen carved by the author in Sycamore.

CARVING A LOGO

W hen I was asked to carve the Guild logo, the first thing I did was look at the reproduction of the subject provided for me to work from. This was 195mm (7⅝in) in diameter.

The prospect was a little daunting. A contributory cause of this condition was my lack of knowledge as to just what the figure shown was at work on.

Carving is by character a very definite process so that the more details one knows about the subject to be carved, the better.

Scaling up the subject to the 380mm (15in) diameter required did help and gave a few more clues to work to.

I do not possess a lathe so that any turning required is done for me by a professional woodturner. The section to which the wood was turned is shown at *fig. 2*.

The material used was Sycamore, a close-grained timber which takes detail well. The colour in this instance was also an asset.

Whilst this process was being worked the lettering was set out and drawn in detail.

Lettering is a very important subject to me, most of my 'bread and butter work' is cutting inscriptions on memorials, or various articles of church furniture, panelling, etc. Boards of various size listing Directors' names for the larger local firms are also sources of such work.

There are many styles of lettering; I use mainly Roman capitals unless a full-sized detail in another style is provided by the client.

Fig. 2. Section to which the circular logo is turned. Overall diameter measures 380mm (15in).

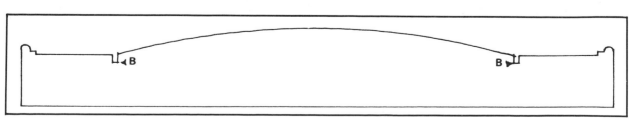

Setting out

Setting out lettering is time consuming, all the more so if it is to be carved around a circle as in the work in hand. However, this was accomplished and transferred to the flat outer rim of the turned matrix. The actual cutting was to be started later and so a cardboard ring was cut out and taped over the set out letters.

Interpretation

The centre now demanded attention. The relevant drawing was used and the lines transferred to the wood using carbon film.

The broken line shown on the illustration gives the foreground limit. The figure and background elements are behind it. This was the first line to be established and after setting in with flat chisels of various widths and a parting tool or two, a small amount of wood was removed on the upper side and the cuts inclined into the line.

Moving on to the figure, the entire seen outline of this was set in including the tools he is using.

These lines are shown by tone applied with a size 'O' sable water-colour brush in the illustration. They were firmly established by setting in with the appropriate tools and the removal of a small amount of wood on the outer side and again inclining the cuts into the line.

In order to have enough room to accommodate the action of the arm wielding the mallet quite a depth of relief was needed. The background level would eventually be taken down to point 'B' on the section drawing *fig. 2* and this was gradually attained. No attempt was made to gain this depth in one clout as it were, but by setting in and removing wood quite a number of times. In other words by steady, controlled progression to within 2mm of the required depth. This amount was required to deal with the wheel and other things hanging on the rear wall.

These were drawn on in their respective positions, set in and the surrounding background taken down to the full depth required.

The textures shown on the printed logo presented a problem; just what did they mean to convey? Why vertical lines on one part and horizontal on another, also what was the darker area against the figure's back?

Eventually I decided to use the texture from shallow gouges to convey these things.

As stated elsewhere, in relief carving things nearest to the beholder are in highest relief, those farther away are in lower relief. With this in mind the forward arm holding the chisel was nearest and in highest relief. The outline of the sleeve was established and the back, the part behind and to the right of the foremost arm was lowered.

Fig. 3. With a cardboard ring taped over the set out letters the drawing is transferred to the wood using carbon film. The broken line gives the foreground limit. The figure and background elements are behind this.

At many intervals throughout the job, the work was placed vertically in a good side-light, and the results observed. This was particularly necessary at the present stage and suggested the next step, the shaping of the three-quarter view of the front of the figure.

In relief a small change of direction in a surface plane can convey a great deal, so small amounts of wood only were removed in progression over this area until the body shape began to be apparent below and behind the left arm.

The jaw-line, chin and cravat were lined in, also the nearer collar and lapel lines. With these in position, the surface was carved to convey the three-quarter front view leaving the lapel as a slightly inclined plane.

The right shoulder and the slightly backward tilt of the forearm, hand and mallet were carved in basic planes only.

The head

When all these things were done the head presented the next difficult problem.

The hat was established in shape, the incline to the under-side of the forward peak indicated and the area of the hair and the facial features revealed below this.

The nearer locks of hair were pressed in with hand-pressure, the temple and cheek levels lowered to the effect of passing under the hair. The forehead was taken back slightly to leave some small projection wherein the nose could be carved later.

The effect was looked at critically once more and the area carried in progression a stage further.

Hands

These are always a problem, how to make them appear to be grasping tools etc., how to obtain the correct angle of the right hand in relation to that which it is holding? All these problems were resolved by working steadily, taking away only small amounts of wood. One could when necessary position one's own hands and look at them in a mirror.

Some sketches or rather scribbles were produced; these are working drawings and are certainly not for display. Maybe only one line from them would in many cases help, but doing them increases awareness of shape, form and the planes necessary to convey those things.

Foreground

The time had now arrived when more sense had to be made of the foreground. The main problem here was to make the wood-bulks appear to be resting on a bench top and to arrive at the incline of the square resting at an angle upon the longer piece of timber being used by the figure.

The square was dealt with by setting in the outlines only and leaving the actual three dimensional effect until later.

The top surfaces of the main bulk were rendered as a plane inclined away from the figure. The vertical face of this was carved at an angle to this down to bench-top level.

The outer two lines only of the smaller bulk were set in and the bench top shown as a plane inclining very slightly away from the viewer towards the main bulk.

This took an awful lot longer to do than to write and constant vigilance of the critical eye was required before the thing looked correct.

Eventually the effect desired was achieved and the various angles of the planes were carved on the bulks of timber to convey their shape.

The edges and top plane to show the construction of the square leaning against the main bulk were carved.

Details

Now details of mallet, hands, the face and hair could be completed. The sleeve-ends with button and button-hole carved and the whole thing gone over, cleaned up and finished.

The final process was the cutting of the lettering, then the job was passed to the polisher for the finishing with french polish as light in colour as possible.

A mirror-plate set into the back and the job set on a screw in the wall, then a final inspection, completed the commission.

FOOTNOTE:
Readers are reminded that the Guild's logo can only be used by registered members of the Guild. For details of Guild membership, write to the Membership Secretary, The Guild of Master Craftsmen, 166 High Street, Lewes, East Sussex BN7 1YE.

NUMERALS

This exercise is intended to be complementary to the previous subject of carved lettering and may be of interest for usage in house numbering.

Western European countries adopted Arabic numerals during the fourteenth century. Roman numerals used prior to this are rather cumbrous in comparison. They may still be used occasionally but have little if any relationship to today's requirements.

There are many ways of depicting the Arabic type now in general use. I know of no set rules governing their shape and proportion. It is more or less a matter of making a personal choice from the many examples to be found in books and other sources.

When writing on the carving of raised lettering, mention was made of 'Gill Sans Serif' as one example of a very legible 'block' lettering style.

The same designer, sculptor Eric Gill, was responsible for an excellent range of numerals. His 'typeface Perpetua', designed in 1925, is a very good example. The only thing I should wish to alter would be the nought.

In this range certain figures project above the general height-line, whilst others descend below the base-line. The object should be to present a good appearance but always to retain legibility. This is easier to accomplish when using numerals only as in the present exercise.

When used as part of an inscription, say for example in dates, ages etc, the figures should be in sympathy with the lettering. This however does not mean that Roman numerals are in any way necessary.

The accompanying illustration shows the type of numeral I have used in such instances over the years. If you refer to this it will, I trust, prove to be more helpful than any wordy description. Keep in mind that the vee-section, and the ruling regarding thick and thin strokes, applies here as in incised lettering.

Should you have any ideas of your own re shapes and pro-

Project: House Numbers

Fig. 1. Outline for a house number to be carved in the style of 'Perpetua'.

Fig. 2. With gouge of appropriate curve the process of setting in of centre lines begins.

portion, try them. Draw them first on paper to clarify your thoughts. As already stated, I know of no strict rulings on the subject and, off hand, can think of no carved examples to which you can be referred.

Church memorials, especially those to be found in church-yards, are not generally of much assistance. The older ones have Roman figures and later ones are poor in the main with the exception of 18th century examples.

Materials and Technique

Any timber used should be of a kind which will weather well outdoors. Elm and oak would be good examples; another would be teak. The latter is notorious for taking the edge off cutting tools, but for the present purpose this should not be considered a very important problem.

Use timber of a size large enough to take the numerals to be cut comfortably and a thickness of not less than 20mm or, say, three quarters of an inch would be most suitable. Plane up the chosen piece and select the face with least amount of figure to be the one used.

Draw the numerals to be used on tracing paper first. This allows for ease of location on the wood.

The size of the figures is up to you. 50mm, 2 inches high would be a good size for clarity. Sizes of less than 25mm, 1 inch in height are not advisable until some experience has been gained.

Spacing

This I have already attempted to deal with in Lettering and the same ideas apply to an equal degree in numerals.

The space between each numeral and its neighbours should be assessed by the eye, not by the use of dividers or any other instrument of measurement. The weight of space within partially enclosed figures, proceeding and following others, should be taken into account when setting out more than two digits.

Procedure

Transfer the numbers to be attempted to the material using carbon paper or film.

Draw in a centre-line to the thickness of each numeral. Sharpen the gouges you will need to set in these centre lines.

Place the appropriate gouge on the curve of the first numeral to be cut and begin the setting-in process of the centre-lines.

The technique of cutting numerals is as that used in lettering. After setting-in remove a little timber with sloping cuts to begin the vee-section required. Gradually work this section to reveal the curves of each figure; remember the flow of these curves.

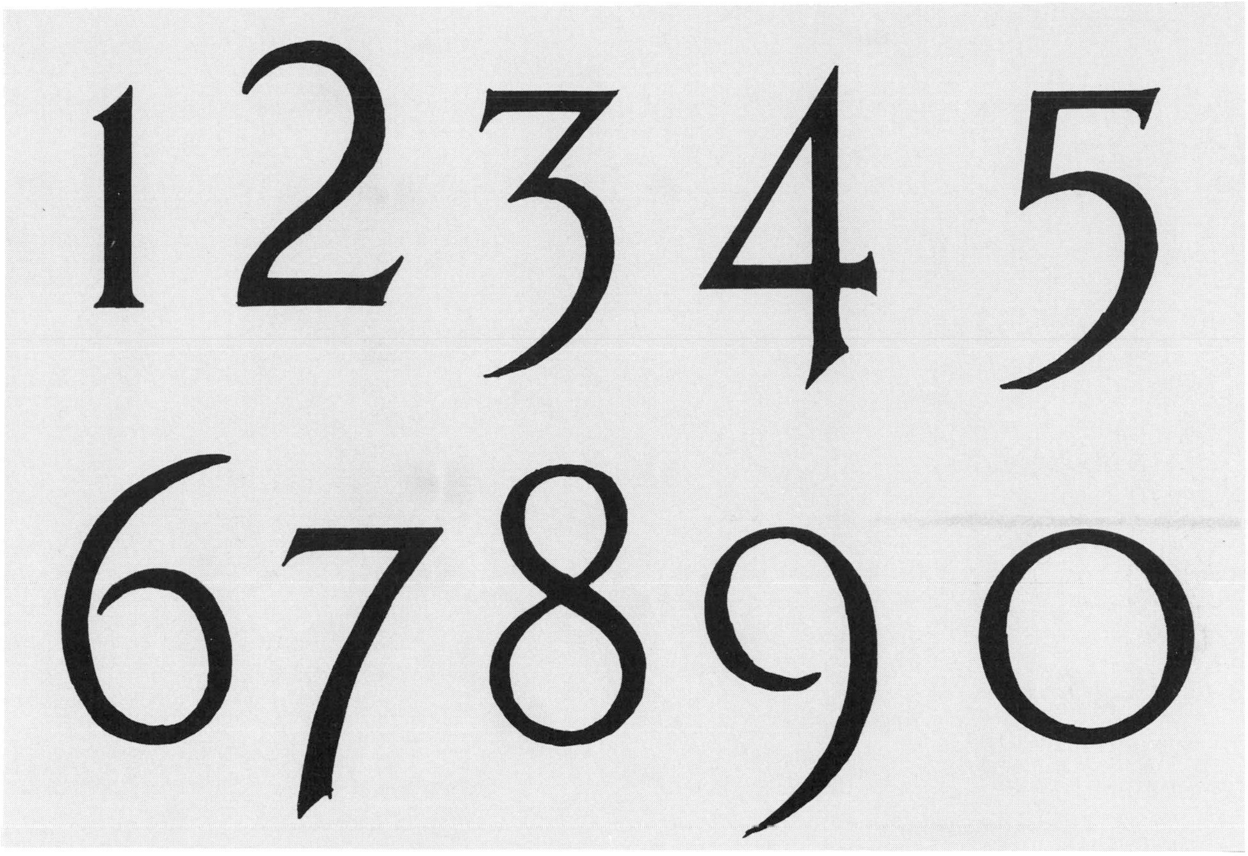

Fig. 3. Numerals based on 'Perpetua' the typeface designed in 1925 by the sculptor Eric Gill. Note how some figures project above the general height line, whilst others descend below the base-line.

The flowing lines are contrasted by straight lines and angles in the numerals one, three, four, five and seven. Be careful, where the vee-section of these strokes meet, to give a clean and clear effect. Keep this clarity in mind when dealing with the serifs to the straight strokes also.

Bear in mind always the sequence of thick and thin strokes explained earlier. If in any doubt, get a pen with a broad nib and write the letter or numeral. A ball-point pen will not give the effect required.

If the work is for outside fixing, some weatherproofing will be necessary. If you use polyurethane, the first coat should be diluted with an equal amount of turps or turps substitute.

This will be absorbed by the timber and when perfectly dry, apply an undiluted coat. Do not allow this to subdue in any way the sharpness of the vee-section. Any accumulation at the bottom of the section will tend to do just that. It is as well to have a small pencil-brush by you, a child's paint-brush, and use this dry to remove any excess from within the vee.

Regarding fixing, this depends on the position and the material on which the plaque is to be mounted. I leave this to you; sufficient to say that the numerals are to be seen not the manner of fixing.

Fig. 1. A design for chipcarving developed by the author from a buckle of Viking origin. The curving lines of the decoration suggest the head of an animal.

ADVANCED CHIPCARVING

With the experience gained when carving the earlier 'chipcarving' project in mind, designs with a less rigid format can now be explored. Designs that is, not relying solely on a geometrical basis.

One architect for whom I once worked, made use of variations on the 'chipcarving theme' to good effect in the decoration applied to various items of church woodwork he designed.

For example, on prayer desks, lecterns and many other such furnishings he was able to gain an effect similar in appearance to medieval tracery. This technique was also a less costly process than the traditional-type tracery would have been.

The idea for this project was suggested by a bronze seen a couple of years ago. This was a grave find that came to light at Vendal in Sweden.

The reference given to this style of decoration is Classic Style II, which is the middle style of three classifications used by Salin, a Swedish archaeologist working earlier this century.

The find, a buckle of Viking origin, has for its decoration shapes which suggest the head of an animal. Working along similar lines I have developed this as an advanced project in chipcarving.

The size should be approximately 180mm (7in) by 155mm (6⅛in) from material not less than 20mm (¾in) thickness.

Material

Japanese oak would suit the subject, Brazilian Mahogany or Beech would also make suitable materials.

Plane the wood up and draw the subject on the best face, being sure to put in the lines shown within each pocket shape.

Fasten the wood down and remember to tilt the cutting edges of the tools being used towards the deepest part of each pocket. Use hand pressure to begin this process of setting-in the lines to the pocket interiors. Once they are lightly indicated, a tap applied by the mallet to the end of the tool handle will give more definition.

Project:
A Decorative Motif

Where three cuts appear within the outline, the point where these meet will be the deepest and the tilt given to the tool's cutting edge as already mentioned will help to give this depth.

In the pockets having four sides, there are two smaller cuts at each end of the roughly rectangular shapes required. These will tilt down to a centre line running between and connecting them, this line will be the deepest cut with the sides and ends cut to make the four sides of the pocket inclined into this.

The ribs of the design will become more apparent as this process progresses. View your work and comparing it with the design when all the pockets are completed, it will be noticed that at certain positions these ribs appear to interlace, passing under or over others.

When this occurs press in the uppermost lines where they cross other ribs. Do this gently with hand pressure only. Then remove a slight amount of wood at these positions from the underpassing surfaces immediately before and slightly incline these surfaces up to the pressed-in lines.

Be careful not to overdo this, only removing sufficient wood to achieve the desired effect of one rib passing under another.

On completion use glass-paper around a flat-faced cork rubber to lightly dress the surface of the wood to remove any construction lines which still remain. Do not use paper of less than 100 grit; 150 grit would be better.

Polish the carving to a suitable finish being careful with the amount of polish used. Polish should not in any way be allowed to 'blind' the sharpness, distinction or depth of any pockets.

Experiment further with a pencil on a pad of unruled paper, drawing shapes with lines overpassing and revealing pockets between the shapes. The field of design is large so have a go and see what comes. If a suggestion of an interesting shape appears follow this up.

Take another sheet of paper and try developing from this suggested shape. Please do not say; 'I can't draw' and simply give up. Try; it is remarkable what can and does materialise from doodles and scribbles.

I say this from long experience of teaching all ages, both young and old who have had this 'I can't draw' fixation.

ADVANCED CARVING IN THE ROUND

Project: A Head for a Rocking Horse

Throughout history mankind has depicted the horse in many techniques and mediums. The earliest of these attempts are those masterpieces of Paleolithic Art found in the areas of France, Spain and also the Tin-Abou Teka in the Tassili area of the Sahara in Africa. These latter have chariots with horses in full gallop beautifully expressed.

The horse occurs in the art of many other ancient peoples. Egyptian and Assyrian sculpture is a rich source, Iran also has a wonderful legacy of such subjects in the reliefs at Persepolis.

The masterpieces of the Imperial Mughal School of Painting, produced in 16th and 17th century India, are among my favourite interpretations. These artists left the world a great legacy of beauty. The heads of their horses are given an elongated simplicity which I find very appealing.

Material

Lime is probably the most responsive material for the present task of carving the head of a horse. From other sources of information on the actual making of a rocking horse, a wood with more tensile strength will be seen to be better for the legs. The rockers will certainly require this quality which is to be found in Ash, Beech and other timbers. I leave the consideration of these points with you and deal here only with the actual carving of the head. Another thing in favour of lime is that it takes colour well.

Procedure

The outline of the head will have to be extended to include more of the neck if it is your intention to use the work as part of an actual rocking horse. See *fig. 2*.

To further assist, I have also made the macquette shown in the photograph. Macquettes – small sketch models of the subject to be carved – are a great aid in establishing the main masses and planes of an idea before embarking on a carving in the 'round'. It's a bit like doodling in three dimensions.

The macquettes I use are generally only about two or three

Fig. 1. The horse in Mughal painting c. 1590. A striking example of elongated simplicity.

*Fig. 2. Head and neck outline drawn
¹/₃rd full-size. Extend to include more of
the neck for mounting on a rocking horse
'body'.*

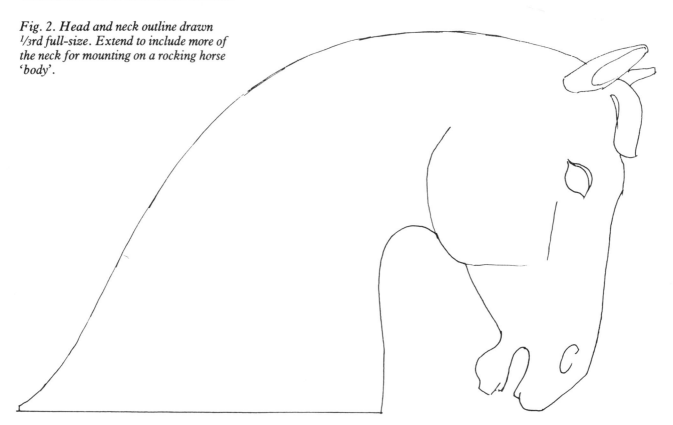

*Fig. 3. Macquette modelled in plasticine
on a copper-wire armature.*

inches high at the most, modelled in plasticine on a copper-wire armature and they do allow some latitude.

Alterations can be made until the idea 'clicks'. They are also useful in giving a good idea of the size of material required for the carving. By scaling-up one arrives at the appropriate size and also the thickness of the timber needed: the latter being a dimension not always easy to arrive at by drawing alone.

Assembly

Returning to the question of carving, a considerable saving in timber and energy can be achieved by assembling the block for the head should the work be of rocking-horse size.

This is done by assembling pieces first cut to their approximate size and shape by bandsaw, bowsaw, coping-saw, or any other means at your disposal.

Modern adhesives are of great assistance when such a block has to be assembled. If the work is to become part of a future rocking-horse, a painted finish will help disguise any differences of grain figuration in the various blocks used.

The block assembly drawing gives a suggestion for the sizes used. At the above size material ex 76mm (3in) and ex 25mm (1in) in thickness would be used.

If the ear-blocks are set at an angle the grain will run along

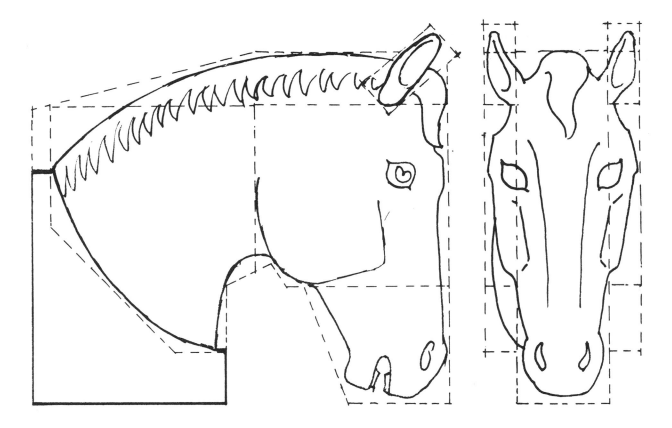

the length of the ears. By this means additional strength will be given to what could otherwise result in easily broken appendages.

In the remainder of the blocks, please try to arrange that the grain all travels as near as possible in the same direction. Try a small cut or two on each piece (not on jointing surfaces).

The piece to the neck and rear is extended to form a holding-piece while carving is in progress. If this is retained and cleaned up on completion it will form the suggested support down to the base. The base itself is a separate and wider piece of possibly contrasting material.

Should you have other ideas for a base, try them.

For the purpose of a carving exercise, a size of, say, twice the size of the Design sheet drawing will be sufficient. This gives overall sizes of 230mm (9in) wide by 190mm (7½in) in height, the tips of the ears will protrude a little above this.

Fig. 4. Block assembly in relation to the outline of the carving. Scale drawn ⅓rd full-size. Try to arrange so that the grain of blocks travels as near as possible in the same direction.

Profiling

At this size the central piece, the core of the material as it were, will be Ex 50mm (2in) thickness, profiled as near as possible to the outline of the side elevation. See *fig. 5*, 'Profiling'. This does of course include the holding-piece.

The cheek-pieces need only be of around 15mm (⅝in)

107

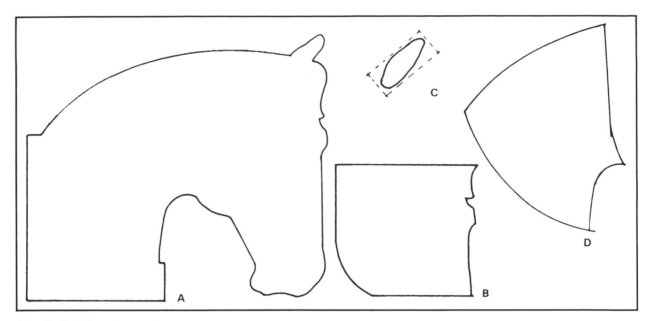

Fig. 5. Profiling shapes prior to assembly: B – Cheek pieces; C – Ear pieces; D – Neck piece.

thickness. These should next be profiled as should the two ear-pieces. See 'Profiling' B, C and D.

Prepare the faces for jointing and assemble the block as shown in the relevant drawing.

Another approach at this size would be to carve the work from one thickness of wood cut to profile A. This however pre-supposes that you are able to obtain wood of thickness of around 82mm (3¼in) finished, i.e. planed-up.

It would probably be as well here to deal with the subject as carved from one thickness. If you choose to assemble the block as suggested you will have less wood to remove by gouge when carving the sides of the head. The next task is to complete the profiling of the side elevation.

Some parts of this outline, such as the underside of the bottom jaw, may prove to be awkward to deal with. These positions can be helped by using a brace and bit or a drill, should you have one, which takes a large diameter flat bit.

Holes are drilled along the outer side of the outline either in sequence or at the position shown in *fig. 6*. Also around lower jaw-line, ear and forelock. These may later be linked by saw cuts.

The holes help the saw to negotiate the changes of direction of the cuts and give a cleaner effect where these occur.

Another awkward part of the outline, if you have no band-saw or such, will be the ears and fore-lock positions.

This problem can be eased a little by making saw-cuts in from the edge of the block across the thickness. See *fig. 6*.

The position and direction of these cuts for the ear and forelock and also the drill centres are shown on this larger drawing.

The sizes of the holes are as follows: No.5 ⅜in Diameter; No.6 ⅜in Diameter; No.7 ¼in Diameter; No.8 ¾in Diameter; No.9 ⅜in Diameter; No.10 ¾in Diameter or metric equivalents.

Use these methods at any other parts of the outline where you consider it could assist you.

Gouges now come into use as the profiling process is continued. The gouge section, size and shape will be dictated by the amount and shape of the wood to be removed at any one position. Deeper, more curved sections will remove wood quicker, but do not let your enthusiasm overcome discretion when using such tools.

Watch the line, remembering always that it is easier to take off than to replace timber.

Leave the mouth area for now and keep the lips linked. The open mouth can be dealt with later.

When profiling is completed, including the base support (holding-piece), the actual 'exploration of form' can begin.

Roughing Out

The first thing to do is draw a centre-line around all the edges of the profiled block. This is most important.

It is also important when working in the 'Round' to realise that material removed from one side of the subject has an effect on the appearance of the whole. Keep this in mind and try not to work for too long on one side only.

Carve one stage at a time and then where – as it will be in the present subject – the problem of balance is important, carve that stage on the other side of the subject. Balance, here meaning the forms found on either side of the centre-line.

Viewing the work from the front will show that the widest parts occur at the ears and at the bone over the eyes. This shows on the front elevation and also on the block assembly drawing.

The drawings show also the general inward slope of the shapes towards the base of the nose. There is a slight fullness at the lips, but the basic shape is a general narrowing.

Another similar but quicker incline begins above this bony structure of the brow and travels towards the crown of the head. If the terms used are not truly 'horsey', please excuse, my daughters are the family experts on such not I.

The ear-shapes springing from this region do attain full block-width and care must be taken to isolate the material necessary for carving them. The slope mentioned above by-passes the ear.

The cheekbones are two plates underlying the surface but having a pronounced effect on the surface form. It is perhaps best to think of them indeed as plates.

A saw-cut across your wood at a point just below the emergence of the ear from the skull, 7mm, (¼in) deep will begin the process. Draw a line across about 16mm, (⅝in) below and parallel to this cut. Then carve an inclined plane using this line as a starting point and ending at the bottom of the saw-cut.

Re **planes**: Perhaps I should repeat here that a **plane** is only a surface. It may be flat, inclined, curved, concave or convex and may travel in any given direction.

Our next task is to establish the jaw-line. Find the gouges of suitable section to fit this line curving across the neck and sharpen these if necessary.

For the present set in these lines only very lightly. At the higher part, the curve joins the upper flow of the neck and any excessive depth will show as a black line where such is certainly not required. The deepening of such lines will be explained later when dealing with the plate-like areas to the sides of the head.

Remember, always incline the tool in use very slightly so that the cut makes a buttress effect sloping away from the higher portion – in this instance the cheek surface. This slope should only be very slight.

I find that if this buttress approach from higher to lower surfaces is not stressed, undercutting invariably occurs leading to complications as the carving progresses.

Perhaps the best way to explain the above is to relate it to edges of cliffs. The sea working at the base of these causes crumbling above and rock-falls. Undercutting, like the sea action, means that surface forms tend to overhang. Changes in shape therefore occur along any such edges as the carving progresses.

Any straightening up can be done later. Undercutting should be kept to a minimum and if at all necessary only done in the final stages of any work.

When the jaw-line is lightly set in remove a little wood on the neck side, cutting down very slightly into the set-in line using a gouge no deeper than No. 4 section. This will give a little more definition to the line. Do this at both sides of the head.

Working a little farther away from the line at its lower curve begin to remove more wood, working back until the position of the broken-line on *fig. 8* is reached.

View the effect of this and working in a similar manner but changing the direction of cuts as the wood directs, continue this shaping. The aim is to arrive eventually at the rounded form shown in the neck-section *fig. 7*. But for the time being just remove some of the excess and take the shape further later.

If the resulting surface looks too rough for you, go over it with a No. 3 gouge until a smoother surface is achieved, do not think yet of the finished surface, the shaping hereabouts will have a long way to go before that stage is reached.

The plate-like areas

Turning now to these large reasonably flat areas which occur at each side of the head, establish the line to the bottom of these.

Do not set in these lines, but rather arrive at them by using a reasonably deep gouge, section No. 6 or 7. Cut a groove or channel just below the line required. The upper side of the groove will then become the lower line of the plate.

The rounded bottom of the groove results in a better transition from the higher plate-like mass to the lower level nearer the nose than setting in the line and then carving up to it would give. It also obviates any persistent black line such as was mentioned earlier. Below these plate-like areas, extending from the curve of the channel bottom, are inclined planes extending towards the corners of the mouth.

These, occurring at each side of the head, result in the narrowing of the face when viewed from the front. There is an amount of thickening when the mouth area is reached, but the overall effect is this narrowing. Continue working in the area to achieve this. Possibly working across the grain will help.

Use about a No. 6 gouge, 10mm (⅜in) wide to define the corners of the mouth leaving a good amount forward to form this. This groove also provides a stop for the inclined planes above.

These gouge cuts should die out towards the portion below which will later become the end of the nose and the muzzle.

A smaller, shallower groove should be cut over each nostril, leaving an amount of surface surrounding these. This will be dealt with as a later development.

Be careful; it is better by far to leave a little too much wood here for such development than to skimp and have too little. Thin nostril edges are not required.

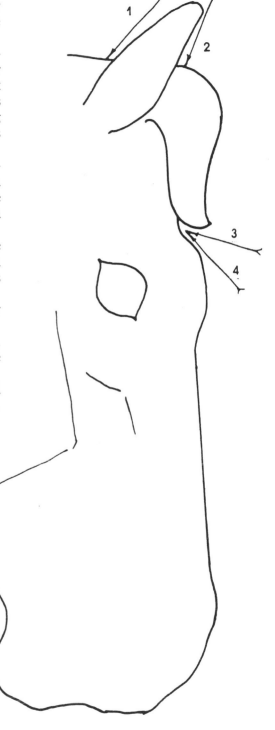

Fig. 6. *To assist in profiling, drill holes at positions indicated and link up with saw cuts.*

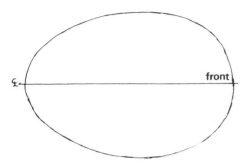

Fig. 7. Section through neck. Care must be taken regarding lines and surface transition.

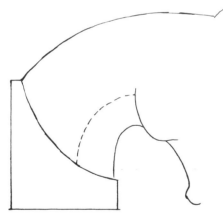

Fig. 8. Dotted line indicates more rounded areas as direction turns under jaws.

Again repeat these cuts on the other side of the head. It is as well at intervals, to take the work to a window – or indeed to any other source of light – and turning it in that light observe the development of shapes so far.

Should this inspection reveal anything which indicates to you how to progress further, have a go. If it appears to lead you astray, stop. But it is only by trying to follow any such indications that your own interpretations will develop.

In the naturalistic drawing herewith there is above the bone over the eye a depression causing a shadow. This depression is there because the bone over the eye socket is narrow at that position until it connects with the stronger bone extending from the crown down the centre of the face.

A cavity is formed here being partly ringed by this bone. Over this cavity the skin passes to give the surface a hollow curve. This hollow is important in that it emphasises the structure. Think of it as a concave plane passing from over the brow towards the position of the ear. Use a shallow gouge and carve this hollow, working steadily with plenty of pauses, to observe the effect being produced.

Forward of this part is the front facing central part of the forehead with the forelock overlying this. Treat the forelock as one piece only as shown in the design, not divided as in the drawing.

The forelock is an upstand. Curved and commencing at the back of the ears, it passes forward between them. By removing some of the wood at each side of this upstand, endeavour to centralise the forelock whilst stopping short of the ear masses.

Work at this point exploring and observing the shapes revealed. Look at the various drawings and at the model photograph. By now the bony structure over the eye should be becoming apparent. The eye position below and under this will now require some attention.

Do not concern yourself with details for the present and try only to carve the slightly full planes as shown in *fig. 8*. These will, in turn, provide the position and material to be later developed when carving the eyes.

From the lower curve at the bottom of these planes, slightly concave surfaces lead to the forward edge of the plate areas. Becoming almost flat surfaces as they pass down the top edges of these and on towards the nostrils, terminating in the grooves already carved just above these.

Look at the work in its present stage and correct any defects of balance, making sure that each plane dealt with so far appears on each side of the centre-line.

The surfaces mentioned here have at an angle to them of almost 45° and travelling in the same direction, almost flat planes which connect them with the actual front leading surface of the head as defined below.

Frontal Plane:

This is the surface of the profile forming the front of the head from brow to just above the nostrils. This is almost flat having only a very slight curve, giving a slight fullness to its section. The outer edges of this frontal plane converge slightly from the brow, then pass in very slow curves towards the nostrils but diverging a little just before reaching them . . .

Use shallow gouges to give these planes reasonable surfaces, sections No. 3 or 4 in width appropriate to the task.

From the bottom edge of the plate area, at an angle to that plane beneath the eye area, is another plane. This, or these counting the other side of the centre-line, form the surfaces to the sides of the reduced width and the general narrowing of the front elevation, you have already roughed out.

Go over these surfaces with shallow gouges to get a good flow to the slightly concave planes required here and at the other side of the head.

View your work from all angles, looking for any as yet under-developed parts. Possibly the neck requires more attention to bring it to the section shown in *fig. 7*. If so, continue work here remembering my earlier remarks re lines and surface transition.

At the jaw-line the buttress idea should be kept in mind also, the incline to this being a little more evident. A slight chamfer effect to these upstands of the rear edges of the plate areas will give a fullness of form. The use of a gouge to gain the transition from the base of these into the neck will add to this.

The planes forming the sides to the narrowing of the head having now been dealt with, the next development can be looked at.

This is the part above the chin and is again a plane at an angle of almost 45°. It arises beneath the plate area and passes down skirting the edge of the mouth, sweeping out a little at the chin. Here becoming a slightly convex curve it passes under to form the end of the chin. Again, try working across grain to rough out this plane and again smooth any too obvious roughness with gouges of No. 3 or 4 section.

The Ears

These are perhaps best likened to cone-like shapes which are truncated at an angle. This gives the surface which is hollowed out to form the opening of the ear.

With this in mind continue working at these ears but **do not** attempt a thin section. Your material is wood not metal or flesh!

Whilst at work in this area carry the forelock a stage further. Give it a full curve to the profile section with possibly concave planes to the under side. Explore this for yourself. Your tool-marks may already suggest possible further development.

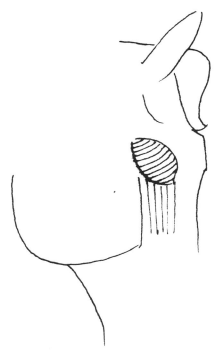

Fig. 9. Detail of eye. Do not hurry the carving process but stand back and observe the result of each cut made. The final result must give the impression the eye could close.

113

Nostrils

Carve a plane at each side of the nose at an angle to the frontal plane. Give these small planes a slight fullness and the nostrils will be carved into these.

The nostrils should be clearly defined – but no quarrying please. Start by carving small indentations to the inverted comma-like shape of these.

Keep looking. If they appear to hold a sufficient amount of shadow, stop.

Work now on that portion of the side elevation which is behind the edge or rim of the nostril and becomes the upper lip. This is a slightly hollow surface which rises gently to form the upper lip leaving a little flat surrounding the nostril. Also, try not to make the lip look too thin.

Mouth

Passing on to the mouth, lightly set in the opening to this. The small curve at the top of this shape, forming the corners of the mouth, is another instance which is best dealt with by drilling a hole. The upper edge of this hole will give the curve needed with less trouble than by carving. Use a 5mm (^{3}/$_{16}$in) drill. Be careful. Do it steadily. Do not cause frayed and fragile edges at the other side by pushing too hard on the drill.

The setting in should be done lightly. Then, taking a little away with a shallow gouge on the inside of the mouth, try to define the upstand of the teeth within this.

The teeth which concern you are at the front only; behind these is the gap for the bit. Do not try for excessive detail here. Suggest, rather than attempt to carve each separate tooth.

If you think that a small amount should be removed by saw, try it. The hole already drilled will receive any saw-cuts made, but do not overdo things. Keep looking as you work and if the desired effect is achieved, stop; leave it.

From this rather lengthy description, and with the drawings before you, you should be able to carry the work forward towards completion.

The Eyes

These are essentially a ball within a socket and the ball is moveable.

Draw, on the surfaces already prepared for them, the shape of the eye. Set in very lightly with gouges of the section shape which best fits the line. Working from within, tip small cuts into the outlines thus defined. Keep looking, and you should see the eye-shape beginnings. Working over the surface gradually, try to carve the curved surface of the eye.

When a satisfactory shape is achieved, think of the eyelids which overlie these and gently set-in the lines of these, giving the cuts a slight incline. Work a little more on the surface of

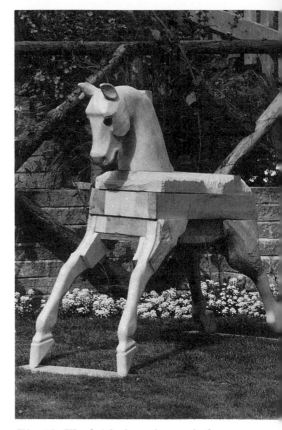

Fig. 10. The finished carving ready for final painting and finishing.

114

Fig. 10. The finished head ready for painting.

the eye, thinking as you do that this surface passes under the lids now set in.

Do not hurry this process. Keep observing the result of each cut made, trying always to keep the cuts under your control.

I've seen eyes carved as two parting-tool cuts over a curve, but there is a lot more to carving an eye than this. Be content to think in the manner described above and progress slowly but always with the work under control.

Perhaps the following may help. I always suggest that students look at their work and ask themselves if the eye they have carved could close. If the answer is no, there is something wrong which must be corrected.

The eyes when completed will appear blind. To enliven eyes a shadow can be introduced. This is done by using a small No. 4 or 5 gouge and pressing in on the eye surface making a segmental shape. A hollow is carved below this to shape the iris, stopping at and leaving this segment remaining.

The light catches this and shadow fills the carved hollow of the iris. The effect can be quite astonishing and is again using the action of light in a similar way to that spoken of earlier.

On a rocking-horse the glass or plastic eyes now available could be used. Be careful when seating these. Don't get them sticking out like 'shuttle-cock nobs'.

ADVANCED PROFILE RELIEF CARVING

Project: A Mask

The present project is to carve a mask of the architectural type. There is no question of hollowing out the back of this, it is for decorative purposes only, not to be worn. The size: as drawn originally 150mm (6in) high × 100mm (4in) wide, ex 50mm (2in thick).

Materials Use a fairly close-grained timber. Lime would be fine for the purpose. Beech is a harder material, but quite satisfying to carve. Japanese Oak is pleasant to cut but the open grain does not really suit the present subject. Poplar, if obtainable, would be suitable.

When material has been selected, draw the full face front view of the design on to it.

Profiling of the front view should be done before any carving of the face is attempted. Working in this way, the block can be held in the vice during the process.

Holding such a profiled piece of wood whilst carving it presents some difficulties. The material could suffer fracture or distortion if an attempt to use the vice was made at this stage.

Some profiled work, if of suitable shape, can be held by means of a backing-piece screwed to the back of the profiled block. However, this must be done with great care, attention being given to the placing of such screws – they must not intrude where carving is likely to take place.

A better and certainly safer method is to glue a sheet of cartridge paper on to the face of a block-board backing piece. This piece should be big enough to take the profiled subject with a margin of surround of a size suitable for a 'G'-cramp. Smooth out all wrinkles and any trapped air pockets and leave until the glue is set.

When this is ready, apply glue to the rear face of the profiled block and fasten this down to the papered surface with 'G'-cramps. Alternatively use your vice if this is deep enough to reach.

Hold the lot in the vice or cramps overnight if possible. Next day the block will be firmly anchored and cramps on the

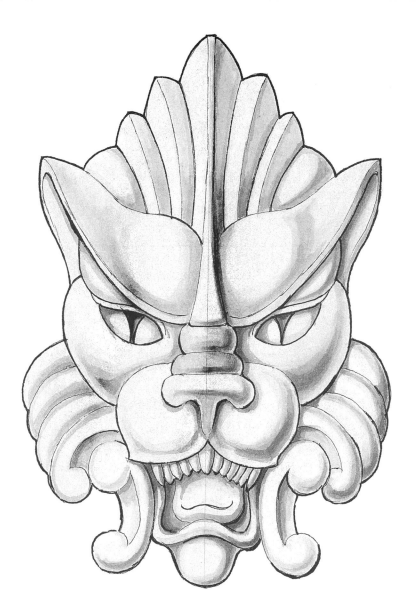

back-board margin will hold the lot securely to the bench top whilst carving is in progress.

The actual profiling prior to this can be assisted by using a saw or by any other means you may have at your disposal. Do this with care ensuring not to intrude beyond the outline drawn on the block.

Carving The highest point of relief will be the tip of the nose and the side view shows a general slope away from this in both directions. The slope towards the top is more gradual but both slopes are interrupted by diversionary shapes.

Use a gouge of medium depth, a number 5 section of about ⅝in width to clear the bulk and go over this with a No. 3 to give a reasonable surface.

The illustration shows this general shaping and the thin broken lines indicate the next stage. For this a number of saw cuts, travelling square across the face at intervals are made.

Figs. 1 & 2. Decorative masks based on animal features such as this are often found in architectural decoration. They sometimes add a mystical aspect to the appearance of a building.

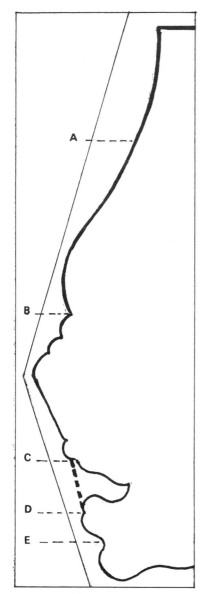

Fig. 3. Side view of the block for carving showing tip of nose as the highest point, and broken lines where saw cuts are travelling square across the face are made.

When the general sloping surfaces are established, put in these cuts with a tenon-saw. Next, working from the highest point of the brow above the eye, cut a slowly curving surface to the bottom of cut 'A'. This will expose the top side of the cut and admit the gouge to remove the remainder, thus continuing this slow curve to the top.

The curve of the brow-line can now be cut. Make this a deliberate curve, be conscious of the curve. This helps the shape, whereas just banging away regardless will in all probability end in a feeble-looking curve and certainly one less bold than it should be. Carry this curve into the bottom of cut 'B'.

Starting now at the highest point of relief and ignoring the smaller curved indentation for the present, carve a slope skirting across the tops of these and ending at saw-cut 'B'

Reverse the direction of gouge cuts from nose-end to 'C' and then on to 'D' leaving the mouth as the broken line shown linking the lips.

Work then from the surface just below 'D' into that cut, leaving a little portion of the general slope surface below. Cut a smaller amount from this, inclining the surface into 'E'. A similar slope below, up into 'E' will commence the chin and the forward edge of this can be dressed back almost to profile line here.

The upstand between 'D' and 'E' will now be seen to be a little high and this can be dressed back just a small amount until touching the bottom lip.

Dress the surface of the chin back to the profile line. You can best assess these positions by using a pair of dividers and measuring up from the back-line of the drawing. Then transfering this measurement using the backboard surface to equal the drawing back-line and marking this height of relief on your block. This method of positioning heights is used throughout the process of establishing the height of relief in this project.

Continue working in this manner until the whole of the front outline is established in the main. The smaller curves of the lips, open mouth and such can be left with a small margin of excess material still remaining at those positions. These will become clearer when the relationship of the forms of the face are revealed in the process of exploring.

That process must now begin and first of all draw a centre-line from top to bottom of the mask following the hills and dales of the shape. Use a soft pencil for this. Use the dividers and measure from this centre-line the widths of the various features. First, the width at the top of the nose and pencil in the shapes, working down this to the nostrils.

The line just at the top of the nose is part of a long curve which sweeps across from ear-tip to ear-tip. Draw this curve on the block, find the gouges of the appropriate slow curve and set in this line.

Remove a little wood on the bottom side of this and vee-in to the line. This will give one of the important lines of the composition. At its centre immediately adjoining the nose this line will have a reasonably vertical upstand to it, with only a very little slope from brow to facial area.

Central to this long curve and from the top of the nose, a long, tapering shape arises and passes back sweeping upwards to the central top-most point. The sides of this are best lined in by using a small parting tool with its vee section.

Only the lower portion of these two lines will be apparent as vee-shapes, above the actual head the lines become central to the decoration. Here they should be kept very shallow, the outer side to each vee will blend with the sides of the central decorative feature above the head-line.

The lines to the tops of the ears which pass along the top of the head to meet the central vee-lines should now be set in showing the limit to the mass of the actual head.

The central portions of these lines are at the top of the curving section between them and the long curve from ear-tip to ear-tip, already set in. This mass is bold in the centre but falls in height towards the ear-tip at each side. Try to carve this fall, working from the high centre out towards the ears leaving about 12mm (½in) of height at the outer edges for the present.

The side elevation shows this fall so have a try at carving this, but keep in mind that this surface is a falling curve, not a flat. Carve the centre portions at each side as bold curves in section, here again a conscious curve gives the better result.

The curves to each side of the nose should now be dealt with and when these small curves are set in, continue the process around the larger and stronger curves of the muzzle. The level around the eye can now be lowered a little at a time, taking off a small amount and then viewing the effect.

The muzzle stands proud of the cheek areas, so remove a little from around and up to the set-in curves of this. The outer lines of the cheeks should also be set in and if the surface of the decorative curves outside these at each side of the head is lowered, this will give a depth to the cheek's curving form which can now be roughed out.

Set in the outer lines of the lower-jaw and lower the level of the curves outside each of these lines.

By now, the whole mask should be taking shape. Stop and look at the result so far. Take to a source of light and turn the carving. Look at the emergence of the forms, if you see a way to improve the effect of these.

Do not try for details yet, just see that the main forms and masses are in effective relationship one to another.

To return to the main curve from the ear-tips, this sweeps down and passes over each eye. To the outer side above the eye and immediately below this main curve is a smaller form,

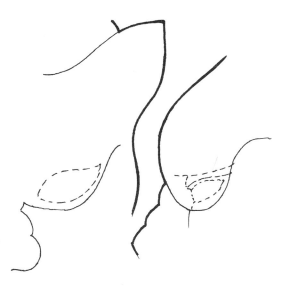

Fig. 4. Broken line shows shape of eye and thickness of eye-lid necessary to create the impression that the lid could close.

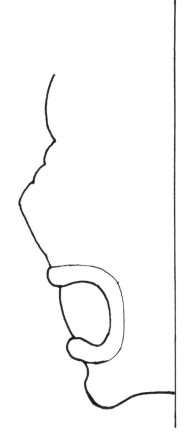

Fig. 5. Shows the teeth, tongue and other forms within as a block filling the mouth, are set back from the lines of the upper and lower lips.

the upper end of which tucks into the opening of the ear. The surface is curved in its longer dimension but also has a curve to its cross-section. At the outer end this curve falls so that its lower edge abuts the upper curve of the cheek.

The curve to the top of the upper eye-lid emerges from under the bottom of this curved form. Set in this curve from the outer edge of the eye-lid up into the ear.

Remove some wood to begin the hollow shape of the ear. Again, working slowly and steadily with frequent pauses to view the effect. The aim is to extend this hollow curved plane until it touches the fuller form over the eye. Look at your work and make sure that all these processes have been carried out on each side of the centre-line.

The Eyes are always difficult to carve and as I have written elsewhere one of the main tasks is to carve them in such a way that the eyelids have some thickness.

With this in mind, carve the eye area, treating it just as a curved surface of sufficient fullness to contain the eye, lids and all. Give this a reasonable surface on which to draw the details of the upper-lid and the eye below this. See *fig. 4.*

Set in the lines drawn and carve the curved surface of the eye and upper-lid as one eye-shaped form for now. Try to give this a clean curved surface and when ready draw on the eye with upper-lid curve passing over this lengthways. Be sure to give the lift to the outer curve-ends. The sight in the eye will be carved last of all, so leave that area for now.

Work now on the forms below the eye areas. These forms are at present only suggested.

Have a further look at the shape of the nose and working from the front, set in the outer shape of this. Remove sufficient wood at each side of this shape to give the required amount of relief, of upstand from the cheeks and the muzzle.

Take the measurements required from the drawing as described earlier and working around these parts, resolve the shapes as in the drawings, roughing out first and then progressing to the details.

When dealing with the nostrils, press the shapes in with hand-pressure only. If you must use a mallet, give light taps only.

The upper and lower jaws should now be thought of as linked forms. Do not, as yet, make any attempt to open them.

When the main shapes here are established draw on the prepared position the lines of the lips and set these in, keeping teeth, tongue and other forms within as a block filling the mouth. See *fig. 5.*

The curves at each side of the mask are suggested by the tufts of hair found here, for example, on the face of a lynx, and have in the design been stylized to decorative curves. These have had a little attention but should now be carried a stage or two further.

Lower the surfaces of these parts at each side of the face using a No. 3 gouge to give a textured surface to the general level, then draw on the lines and set in the lower units only. The shapes of these, which occur at each side of the lower jaw are shown along with a section through the shape in *fig. 6*. Try to carve these to this section.

The recurring curves above the lowest unit show a stepped recession shape in the same figure; carve these to this section.

Turning now to the top of the mask, a similar effect is required but with a greater thickness of material to work on.

Fig. 7 shows the section to keep in mind as you work this part of the subject, the higher crest radiating from the top line of the head proper. The inclined sides to each trough giving a strong light and shade effect.

The Mouth Draw on the surface prepared as *fig. 5* the teeth of the upper jaw making sure that the fangs at each side are stressed.

Should you have a fairly wide, say ⅝in or ¾in No. 3 section gouge, use this to set in the general curve only, to pass along the crown of the teeth. Leave sufficient protrusion at the outer extremes to accommodate the shape of the fangs.

Remember that the teeth are set back from the line of the upper lip, in other words, they must appear to be within the mouth. The lips cover them when the mouth is closed.

Set in the line of the upper lip as it passes over the teeth and lower the surface of the wood below this. In doing so, the general line to the surface of the teeth will be positioned giving an upstanding edge to the top lip above it.

Also set in a little deeper the general curve passing along the crowns of the teeth mentioned above, and draw in the line to the upper surface of the end of the tongue. Using this line as a starting point, work a curved, inclined surface back until it is stopped by the set-in line.

Work over this surface with a gouge of No. 4 section or should you have a spoon gouge, the section curve of which is the equivalent of No. 4, try using that for the purpose. The spoon curvature will help to produce just the curved and inclined plane required for this, the upper surface of the tongue.

To allow the wood being removed here to come away easily, you will have to continually re-set in the general curve to the teeth crowns as described above and pressing it deeper into the mouth. Work at this process steadily, gradually increasing the depth, but removing only a little wood at each cut. Do not try to force the pace of removal or breakages will occur.

Take the wood to the source of light to check progress of the depth carved and the shadow this is producing.

As a result of working in this way, the outer edges of the mouth should stand proud at each side of the tongue. This is as it should be, but refer to the side view of the Mask *fig. 2* and

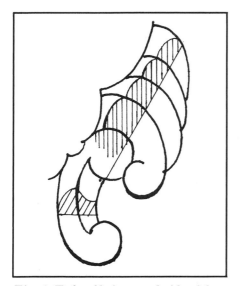

Fig. 6. *Tufts of hair on each side of the mask are suggested by curves in stepped recession. The shaded areas indicate a section through the shape.*

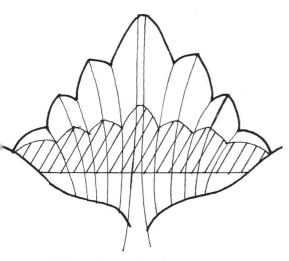

Fig. 7. *Shows how the crest rises above the tops of the ears but forms part of the nose through the long tapering shape in the centre.*

remember that the mouth shape from this view must also be kept in mind.

The lines of the sides of the tongue front view should now be drawn on and these lines carved in carefully with a small parting tool using its vee-section. The curves to the front of the tongue can be set in with the appropriate gouge now and an attempt made to lower the surfaces of the wood between tongue and the lines of the inside of the mouth.

This may set a problem, but this is one instance where a small 'veiner' with its 'U' section will help. There are some available which look in section like the shape across an umbrella rib. I think the section number may be No. 11 but if a small veiner is asked for by name, this should help.

A small 'fluter', i.e. a gouge deeper than a half circle in section shape will help. These can be obtained down to ⅛in in width. Try to carve this margin between tongue and inside of the mouth fairly deep, a strong shadow is needed here.

Work on the lower jaw with the drawing in front of you, try to get the curve under the bottom lip to hold a reasonable amount of shadow. The edges of the rim of the lower-jaw should be flowing curves and have a rounded shape to the section through at any point in their flow.

The Eyes will require more work to complete the surfaces, line of the lids, etc. When you feel that no more can be done here, draw on the eye surface the shape of the 'sight'. This is an inverted triangle and should be dealt with in the manner used earlier to cut the eyes of the head of the rocking horse.

Check your carving as a whole against the designs and the only things remaining to be dealt with should be the teeth.

Draw these on the surface prepared for them and carefully set in the lines. The fangs should rest upon the outside of the mouth at that position. They may be slightly undercut where they touch but do not attempt to free them from that upon which they rest.

Make small vee-lines to establish each tooth and round the surface of each slightly into these. Carve the crowns of the teeth to shape and do any tidying up in that area.

After a final check of the whole project, slip the edge of a flat chisel bevel down to the papered board, against the top-most edge of the carving. Tap gently with a mallet and the carving should lift from the backboard. If it does not, try this procedure at other points of the carving's edge. Not, I must stress, at any places where the wood is too thin.

When the carving is free, wrap a good sized sheet of rough sand paper around a flat board and place the carving papered-side down. Move backwards and forwards over the sand paper until paper and glue are dressed off.

Let a glass plate in the back to hang the carving by. Apply the polish you favour and so complete this quite advanced project.

Ideas for Further Projects

The Human Head

The shapes and forms which compose the human head are varied and diverse. There are of course racial characteristics which add to this diversity.

The Skull is the underlying bony structure, the shape of which must be kept in mind when carving any head. This is shown in the drawing.

The other illustration shows the main planes which, cloaking the underlying bone structure, reveal the basic volumes and three dimensional forms which together compose the head, face and features.

The Forehead has a large curved plane to the front, flanked by the returning planes forming the temples at each side. This shape passing down to the ridge of the brow gives way to the recess below the eyebrows which in turn gives accommodation for the eyes.

The Nose is central to the face and is of a wedge-like shape consisting of three planes, one down the front and having slightly sloping planes passing away from this surface at each side until meeting those of the cheeks to the front of the face.

These cheek planes pass on down to the level of the opening of the mouth. At the base of these are two smaller surfaces which passing forward at a slight incline contribute to the structure of the chin.

The forms necessary to give the shape of the mouth and the area surrounding this are shown.

The Ears, occurring at each side of the head, each occupy a position which can be arrived at by thinking of two lines drawn across each profile of the head. One at the point where the top of the nose begins to project below the forehead and the other drawn parallel to the first passing immediately below the nostrils. The space between these lines will be occupied by the size, the height that is, of the ear.

Hair, this makes a shape which is softer and which encloaks the appropriate portion of the skull.

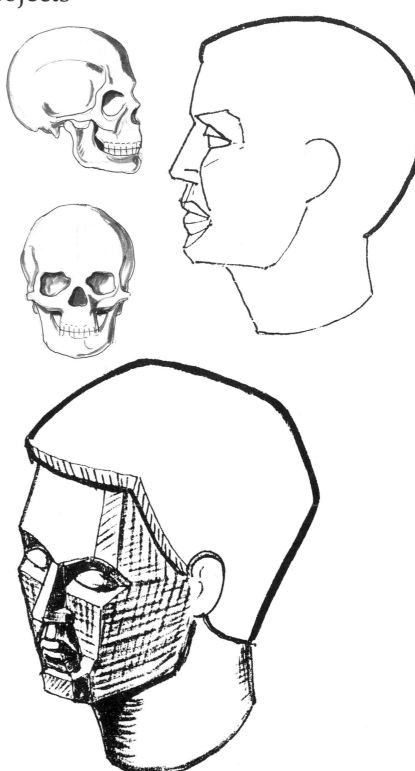

Ideas for Further Projects

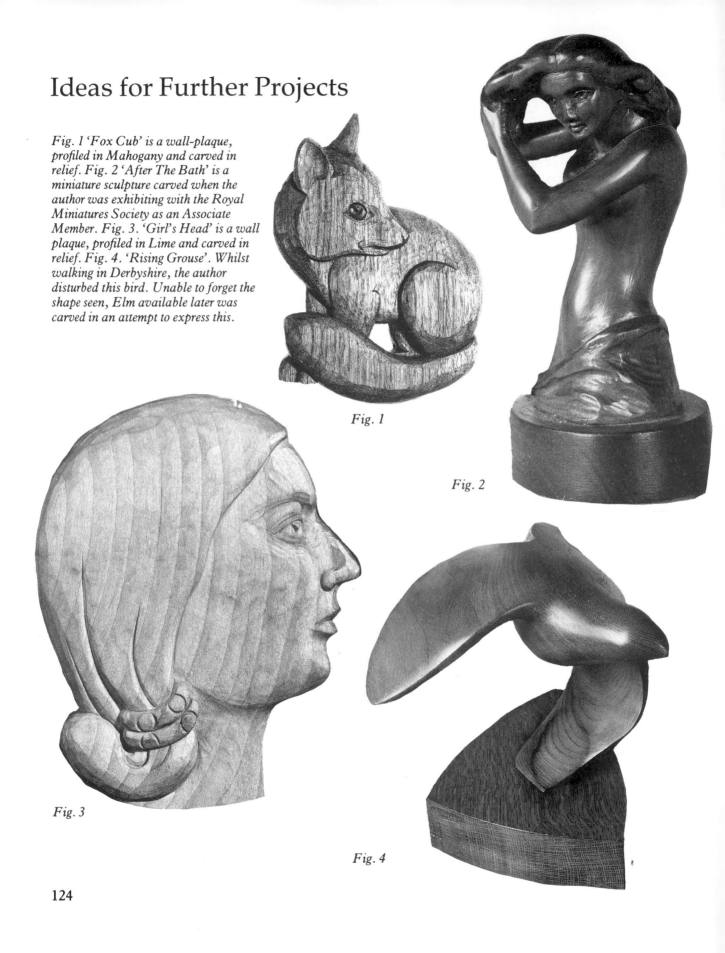

Fig. 1 'Fox Cub' is a wall-plaque, profiled in Mahogany and carved in relief. Fig. 2 'After The Bath' is a miniature sculpture carved when the author was exhibiting with the Royal Miniatures Society as an Associate Member. Fig. 3. 'Girl's Head' is a wall plaque, profiled in Lime and carved in relief. Fig. 4. 'Rising Grouse'. Whilst walking in Derbyshire, the author disturbed this bird. Unable to forget the shape seen, Elm available later was carved in an attempt to express this.

Fig. 1

Fig. 2

Fig. 3

Fig. 4

Fig. 5

Fig. 5. 'Ploughing' – Relief carving in Oak.
Fig. 6. 'Mother And Child'. Carving in the round in Elm.
Fig. 7. 'Fox Cub'. Relief panel in Lime.
Fig. 8. 'Resting Fawn'. Carving in the round in Lime.

Fig. 7

Fig. 8

Fig. 6

WHERE TO VIEW EXAMPLES OF WOODCARVING

In these islands we have a great heritage of beautiful woodwork and a very large amount dates from pre-Reformation times. The medieval craftsmen left examples of their great skill in many places throughout the land.

The Church provided the bulk of opportunities for the exercise and development of these skills.

Regional styles of construction and decoration developed and there are few districts which do not have an old church with interior woodwork of interest to woodcarvers and indeed to many other people.

The actual layout of the church at this stage in its long history gave plenty of scope for carpenters, joiners and carvers. For example, the chancel screen which maintained the traditional seclusion of the sanctuary housing the main altar.

Previous to the 13th century this division of the sanctuary from the main body of the church was more pronounced. Walls provided the division, sometimes with only a comparatively small doorway linking the two parts of the plan.

Later this was widened to eventually become the chancel arch.

The earliest wooden screens were comparatively simple in design and construction; decoration was restricted to tracery as at Addlethorpe in Lincolnshire. Winthorpe in the same county has a parclose screen. This type is used to part enclose areas in the aisles of a church, some of these containing lesser altars.

Later developments were arched screens, Rood screens, and Rood lofts. These latter culminated in the wonderful examples to be found in the West Country.

The Rood is a figure of Christ upon the Cross. The name Rood applied to such a figure is Saxon; these were originally in stone.

One such piece of Saxon sculpture is to be found at Langford in Oxfordshire. This does not occupy its original position now.

With the progression and development of the Gothic style, the pointed arch made wider chancel arches possible.

This in turn led to the development of wooden chancel screens from the 13th century onwards, throughout the three phases of Gothic architecture in Britain.

The Rood flanked by the figure of the Virgin Mary on one side and St John on the other surmounted many of these screens, hence the name 'Rood screen'.

There are some screens existing which have the mortice holes remaining where the Cross and figures were positioned.

Cullompton in Devon is one example. The Rood and all other figures were removed from churches at the time of the Reformation. However, before this, later developments in Gothic screens were the Arched screen, and finally the screen surmounted the Rood loft.

The oldest screens were of quite heavy construction, but later examples are beautiful with a wealth of carved decoration and in some instances fan vaulting to the overhang of the loft to the screen.

Some had painted decorations, saints portrayed on the panels etc., but many such have suffered at the hands of would-be restorers.

Of latter years many churches have become redundant and closed. Although I cannot think such fate will have befallen those mentioned here, it would be wise to check that entry would be allowed before venturing on journeys of any distance.

Also some churches are locked against vandalism, but an enquiry at the Vicarage or Rectory will almost certainly result in the building being opened for anyone who has a genuine interest to view.

So check, possibly by telephoning the Rector or Vicar. Another way is to consult a copy of *Crockford's Clerical Directory*, which generally can be found in the reference department of your local public library. This publication lists all the Anglican Parish Churches, their clergy and other information. The nearest town is generally given as the 'post town'.

The following is a short list (there are many more) of churches with screens of various types and other woodwork. All are of interest to woodcarvers, and indeed to all people with an interest in beauty and craftsmanship.

Addlethorpe – St Nicholas, near Skegness, Lincs. Has tracery of the 'two light' type, also crockets.

Atherington – St Mary, near Barnstaple, Devon. Early 16th century, late Gothic. An excellent West Country type. Possibly the most beautiful one of all. Both the east and west sides of the screen are marvels; the west side is the one facing the congregation, and has a wealth of carved decoration. The screen is vaulted and shows this on either side.

Backwell – St Andrew, lies off the A370 near Clevedon, Somerset. Excellent and is one of the first I remember seeing shortly after demob at the end of the last war.

Beverley Minster – Yorkshire, East Riding. Has marvellous stallwork among its many treasures.

Chester Cathedral – Has many treasures, the stall canopies dating from the late 14th century are wonderful.

Christian Malford – All Saints, south of Malmesbury on A240, Wiltshire. Unusual in having the inverted cresting of the upper portion turning a quarter circle down at each outer-end

The pulpit in All Saints Church, Kenton, Devon. Late 15th century. Described as 'High Gothic' some panels show paintings of saints.

where it reaches the wall. The triangular shapes left by this each have an elaborately carved spandrel.

Chulmleigh – St Mary Magdalene, south of South Molton, Devon. Late 15th century.

Derwen, Clwyd – St Mary, south of Ruthen, Denbighshire. Has screen, open panels with tracery heads.

Dunster – St Georges, near Minehead, Somerset is vaulted. Screen with cresting, Bressumer and tracery heads.

127

Flamborough – St Oswald, near Bridlington, East Riding of Yorkshire. (As a Yorkshireman the new designation of North Humberside gives me the creeps.) This screen is late 15th century and has a Rood loft.

Halse – St James, is west of Taunton, Somerset. Has 15th century screen.

Handborough – SS Peter and Paul, Oxon. I think the actual name may be Church Handborough, has a screen in the north aisle. This church also has a traceried pulpit.

Kentisbeare – St Mary, near Cullompton, Devon. Late 15th century. Screen has marvellous Bressumer decoration.

Kenton – All Saints, south of Exeter, Devon. Has a beautiful screen and also an outstandingly beautiful pulpit.

Keynsham – St John the Baptist, near Bristol, Somerset. In 17th century, the tower fell smashing the chancel screen, some parts remain. It has a good Jacobean pulpit.

Lapford – St Thomas of Canterbury, near Crediton, North Devon. This Rood screen is a marvel, extending across the interior width of the church including the north aisle. Early 16th century, one would find it a hard job to decide whether **Atherington**, already mentioned, or this one is the most beautiful screen in Britain.

Llananno – St Anne, is just north of Llandridod Wells.

Llanrwst, – Denbighshire, is vaulted and beautiful. An unusual feature is that in addition to the usual vine decoration running throughout its full width, it has a smaller running design of oak. This is oak seen with a designer's eye, not any slavish attempt to copy nature; the result is grand.

Milverton – St Michael, is near Taunton, Somerset. Has a late medieval bench-end which shows Renaissance influence.

Mobberley – St Wilfred, near Knutsford, Cheshire. c. 1500. An arched screen of North Country type.

Poltimore – St Mary, north east of Exeter, Devon. An outstanding example of the late Gothic period, indeed the decoration on the panels between the vaulting ribs shows the advent of Renaissance-style ornament. The idea of decorating panels in this position occurs on other screens, but on no other to such an advanced transition of style. For example **Ashby St Legers**, Northants, where the decoration is tracery.

Plymtree – St John the Baptist, near Cullompton, Devon. An arched type with vaulting. This screen also crosses the entire width of the church interior. This has tracery decoration between the ribs of the vaulting.

Southwold – St Edmund, King and Martyr is on the coast in Suffolk. It has an 'arched'-type screen in the East Anglian style.

Swimbridge – Devon. Has a chancel screen with early 16th century decoration.

York Minster – York. A treasure house with many wonders. If you go, try to see the carved chest which has a high relief carving of George and the Dragon on its front.

If you live near or are in the vicinity of any of the above-mentioned churches I strongly advise a visit.

You will in many cases have to approach the clergy to open the church; it is a sad commentary on our times that they have to be locked at all.

However, do not let this put you off, people with genuine interest will find a welcome I am sure.

If you visit any of the Medieval Cathedrals remember to look at the Misericords to be found under many seats in the choir. These could form a subject for study of their own.

Norfolk and Suffolk abound in wonders, some of the font covers are exquisite. This area also has some marvellously roofed interiors, some having angels to the Hammer-beams.

The list could go on and on, so wherever you may be in Britain, spare a little time to visit the local churches.